AF479133

THE TRADITION OF FINE BOOKBINDING IN THE TWENTIETH CENTURY

The Tradition of Fine Bookbinding
in the Twentieth Century

CATALOGUE OF AN EXHIBITION

12 November 1979 to 15 February 1980

COMPILED BY BERNADETTE G. CALLERY & ELIZABETH A. MOSIMANN

ESSAYS BY JEAN GUNNER, BERNARD MIDDLETON & MARIANNE TITCOMBE

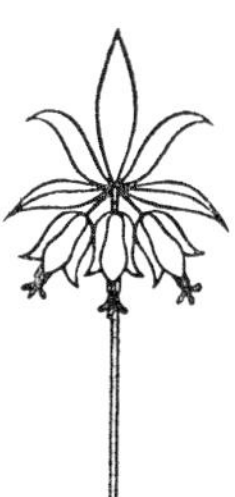

HUNT INSTITUTE FOR BOTANICAL DOCUMENTATION

CARNEGIE–MELLON UNIVERSITY

AND DAVIS & WARDE, INC.

PITTSBURGH, PENNSYLVANIA

1979

4

Text set in 10 and 14 point Bembo Monotype and
printed letterpress on Hunt Curtis No. 2 mould-made
paper by Davis & Warde, Inc., Pittsburgh.

Color separations by Pittsburgh Atlas Photoengraving Co.

Photographs by Alan Cherin Studios, Pittsburgh, unless
otherwise credited.

Designed by Rob Roy Kelly, assisted by Jean Gunner,
Frances Hannan and Henry M. Yocco.

ISBN 0-913196-28-2

The Tradition of Fine Bookbinding in the Twentieth Century explores
the tension that results from modern craftsmen working in a traditional craft.
The twentieth century binder must always contend with traditions of
binding structure, material and cover design, and this conflict is compounded
when facing the re-binding of an older book.

We have attempted to gather representative examples of what we see as
the two major divisions of modern binding: the traditional or retrospective
approach, and the modern design or intuitive approach where the design
is intended to be an expressive extension of the book within. Such distinctions
are somewhat arbitrary, and the binders are even less easily categorized
than their bindings. Retrospective bindings need not be restrictively imitative.
And binders frequently look to historical styles for inspiration even when
creating new designs that reflect the artistic tastes of the twentieth
century. The requirements of the book itself should also determine some
aspects of the binding. All works of value deserve a careful choice of conservation binding techniques. The exquisite twentieth century *livre d'artiste*
and the primary scientific source of the eighteenth century demand equal
respect, though different design considerations.

Our survey includes selected original examples of major historical styles,
countered with a variety of twentieth century bindings, both modern and
retrospective. By grouping the bindings according to style, we hope
to demonstrate relationships in design and technique which suggest that no
modern binder is beyond tradition.

ACKNOWLEDGMENTS
We wish to thank our lenders, whose generosity has enabled us to strengthen
our stylistic comparisons with significant bindings. Curators who have
been notably liberal in sharing their expertise, as well as their treasures, include
Anne Skoog of the Hunt Library, Robert Nikirk of the Library of the
Grolier Club, and Paul Needham of the Pierpont Morgan Library. The collectors Kulgin Duval and Colin Hamilton have greatly assisted us in locating
bindings which have passed through their hands. Valuable information

and counsel have been received from Mirjam Foot and Anthony Hobson, and from Bernard Middleton and Marianne Titcombe, who also contributed essays to this catalogue. Discussions with the contemporary binders Edgar Mansfield, Philip Smith and Ivor Robinson have aided us in understanding the interrelation of theory and technique.

As for our colleagues at the Institute, we are grateful for the tolerance and goodwill shown us during the preparation of this catalogue and exhibition. Our thanks are particularly due to Robert Kiger, for his editorial persis-

tence, to John Brindle, for his ingenuity in solving many problems of the
exhibition, and to Donna Connelly for deciphering and typing many
drafts of the text. Jean Gunner wishes to thank Olivia Primanis Cherin, Sally
Ketchum, Julia Miller and Ellen Owings, for their practical assistance.
Of Jean Gunner, our binder, we can say entirely without cliché that without
her, the exhibition would have been impossible.

We remain indebted to the generations of known and unknown craftsmen who have maintained the tradition of fine bookbinding.

An exhibition such as this performs a valuable service in that it helps to
create public awareness of bookbinding and may lead some to further study
of the craft's many complexities and wide range of types and grades of
materials. It should also be of benefit to many who are responsible for the
care of books, whether they be housed on a few feet or several miles of
shelving. Far too much binding and repairing is at present being commissioned
without searching questions being asked; indeed, in my experience
it is rare for collectors, librarians and dealers handling books worth scores of
thousands of dollars each to show even slight interest in, for instance,
the structure of the binding, reinforcements used in repair work or the quality
of the materials to be used.

Perhaps, too, those who own or are in charge of book collections will be caused
to think objectively about the style of binding employed on their books,
and they may want to reconsider their approach to decoration. Should
early books be put into pastiche bindings; should bindings be clearly modern
but reminiscent of the period of the books, or should they be unequivocally of
our own time? The occasion of this exhibition provides a rare opportunity
to weigh up the pros and cons and decide.

Three main activities are open to the modern binder who is concerned
with fine work, and he may opt to engage in any or all of them—the repair
or restoration of books and bindings, the rebinding of antiquarian books,
and the binding of modern books. The first category is outside the scope of
this exhibition, but it is important work calling for special skills, especially
when it is restoration rather than repair. The second area of activity, the
rebinding of old books, is contentious. Those who work for collectors and
dealers are, on the whole, required to rebind books more than about one
hundred years old in the style of the period to which they belong, and as
authentically as possible because anything not strictly in period offends the
patron's sensibilities, and a binding very much out of keeping may well
reduce the market value of the book. There are good arguments for and
against this approach. One can say that however good the pastiche, either the
materials or subtle points of technique will betray it, but as they are not

obvious, the owner feels easy with it and there is no deception or harm. Those
who are opposed to this policy feel that there is no justification, moral or
aesthetic, for attempting to make a binding appear to be what it is not,
even if deception is not intended or likely. The much-favored alternative in
many libraries, where personal pride and other considerations of the collector
do not obtain, is to rebind books published before our own time, especially
those printed several centuries ago, in a style which is neither deceptively
ancient nor blatantly modern, but is no more than reminiscent of the date and
place of publication. Such is the policy of the Hunt Botanical Library. The
third area of activity is the rebinding of modern books. If the modern books
are reprints of earlier ones, the binder enjoys rather more latitude than he
would if the books were the original editions. Whether or not he has com-
plete freedom is again debatable.

In recent decades craft bookbinding has changed greatly both in the United
States and in Britain, and on the whole the changes have been for the
better. Output per man and the level of sheer manipulative skill have dropped
everywhere because, among other reasons, there is now less subdivision of
labour. At one time, less than sixty years ago, armies of men churned out
beautifully produced but very stereotyped bindings, most of which were
destined to be "furniture." The market for this has all but vanished, though
recently Arab money has, possibly temporarily, reversed the trend. Today, with
more important work to do, we need binders, repairers and restorers
equipped not only with a broader range of skills but possessed of an analytical
turn of mind, a knowledge of materials and an interest in the past, both of
the craft and generally. Without the interest, restored bindings and also
new ones, whether or not they are intended to be pastiches, tend to look and
feel "wrong," however skillfully the work has been done.

Repairing and rebinding books of earlier periods is the bookbinder's most
important function today and the enormity of the task confronting him
is awesome. Scores of millions of books are deteriorating at a compound rate,
by which I mean that the rate of deterioration increases as condition worsens. It
is sobering to speculate that one book which needs to be deacidified,
resized and rebound or repaired may well occupy one hundred hours of skilled
time, and if paper-mending is involved, the expenditure of time is likely
to be very much greater, and yet there are comparatively few binders qualified
to handle the work unsupervised, as many have to.

Bookbinding retains in many minds an unfortunate image associated with one's
aunt, who, many years ago, did simple bookcrafts at evening classes.
In reality, the craft is an extremely difficult one to master, partly because each
binding involves at least forty skilled operations, most of which depend
for their success on the success of the previous operations. Also, it involves the

use of several unstable materials which behave in different ways when initially used, and to some extent behave unpredictably in subsequent environmental conditions. Other important, complicating factors are that various qualities of these materials have varying working characteristics and life expectancies.

The present-day binder needs to be versatile because not many establishments can support specialists, and he must be flexible and innovative because every book has its peculiarities and presents a different problem. In the past, when most work went through trade binderies, there was a tendency to force books into one or another of a number of set styles of binding with varying amounts of decoration for each. The style one chose depended not so much, as it should, on the physical nature of the book, as on the amount one wished to spend or the effect one wanted on the bookshelf. Therefore, a style which was appropriate and cheap would not be employed because it did not look imposing. The work was executed by large bindery staffs with considerable subdivision of labour, so that one man would execute but a small part of the whole, and inevitably under those conditions would give the job little objective thought. Even if this had not been the position, the craftsman would have had little latitude or opportunity to suggest divergences from the norm.

Today, in Britain, the situation is changing, and changing for the better. The quality of trade firms' intake of labour remains much as it used to be from the educational standpoint, and that is not high, but it seems to me that the standard of education of non-trade binders, which has always been higher than that of trade craftsmen, is rising and the numbers involved are rapidly increasing. The quality, intellectually and otherwise, of the intake of labour in both America and Britain is very good, which is an immensely encouraging factor for the future. A good intellect and conscientious motivation are essential prerequisites for today's binders and conservators, and will be needed increasingly as the years pass and as the condition of books in general worsens and treatment becomes more complicated and scientific.

In Britain, and probably in America, the greatest amount of routine work comes from book dealers. Less is commissioned by collectors, probably because, in the case of the more valuable books, the work has been done before they are offered for sale. Until recent years a substantial amount of repair work was forthcoming from small collectors, but the financial position of the middle classes in Britain has significantly worsened, while at the same time the prices of antiquarian books have risen sharply, far outstripping the Cost of Living Index. Thus, many have been forced to abandon serious collecting, or have reduced their level of collecting and have stopped having their books repaired and rebound. Most learned societies and public institutions have extremely limited funds, so unless a grant is forthcoming from a charitable foundation, the amount of work is trifling and such money as is available seems to be spent on the binding of periodicals. There are, however, notable exceptions, especially among the older universities. The richer institutions often have their own binderies and the less well endowed seem to give preference to the acquisition of more books.

In Britain, in recent years, commissions for designed bindings have come principally from a few discriminating dealers. One thinks immediately of Messrs. K. D. Duval and Colin Hamilton who courageously commissioned twenty-three binders to produce nearly forty elaborate bindings in 1974-1975, carefully selecting certain books for particular binders. Mr. Colin Franklin and others have also given vital assistance to the craft by commissioning binders and by purchasing bindings at exhibitions. The commissioning of binders is the more important policy for the future of the craft and for the satisfaction of the craftsmen because it enables them to bind books of merit and value. Few craftsmen can afford to bind valuable books speculatively with the attendant risk of not finding a purchaser for several months or even years. Even binding a valueless book without a commission can be a financial strain. Although on both sides of the Atlantic there are collectors who have assembled large numbers of modern bindings it is difficult to think of any who can be regarded as a latter-day Grolier or Mahieu, both of whom in the sixteenth century commissioned many bindings. Notwithstanding this and the fact that the amount of fine binding now being produced is only a small fraction of what it used to be, the creative, non-trade side of the craft has blossomed during the last fifteen years or so, and I am prepared to say that it has more adventurous vitality, intellectual creativity and diversity of styles and approaches than ever before.

The craft's potential market is enormous. Fine binding could "take off" at any time for no apparent reason as other crafts have in recent times, and become very fashionable, but steady growth would be better for the craft than the sudden mushrooming which enables charlatans to flourish. A boom would be short-lived anyway because demand could not be met, backlogs of work would be lengthy and interest would die after a year or two. One potential source of work is the almost unlimited scope for V.I.P. visitors' books for large commercial concerns, liners, clubs and many other bodies which can easily afford them. Many already have off-the-shelf traditional-style books, but few think of commissioning bindings which would be unique, appropriate to the organization and prestigious.

At present, the public at large is not conscious of bookbinding, especially modern designed bindings, because examples are seldom to be seen anywhere, unlike paintings, prints and sculptures. Why is the craft, outside France, known to such a small circle, and why is it such a struggle to get it recognized

as a major creative craft, a craft which arguably has more to offer than
any other? And why is it that designs on book covers are not taken as seriously
as those which appear on canvas and paper? There are many possible answers;
one, I believe, is that for a relatively obscure craft it is expensive, necessarily
so, and becomes alarmingly costly when 40% or more commission is added by
commercial galleries. Also, in most countries fine binding has a very short
tradition as a really exciting, thought-provoking medium for design. It was
largely traditional and up-dated pattern-making until thirty years ago
when Edgar Mansfield burst upon the scene with his concept of expressive
design. Bookbinding design which engenders excitement and has an intellectual content is therefore still a fairly new field of activity, so it is scarcely
surprising that it has not yet become fully recognized.

It is hard to believe that bookbinding will not soon be taken seriously here
as it is in France, because it has so much to offer, as is evident in this exhibition.
For a start there is the book itself, and then there are the subtleties of the
binding's functional relationship with the physical nature of that book. Very
many factors are involved which can make the whole a delight to handle
or make it a clumsy, unuseable monstrosity. A knowledge of these
multifarious points can immensely increase the pleasure of ownership and help
to raise standards. The binding can incorporate many attractive and interesting materials with a great range of grains, textures, colours and decorative
effects. The subtleties of design are endless and may involve deeply pene-
trative interpretation of the author's theme and approach, or the design may
produce an effect which almost indefinably has a link with the subject or
atmosphere of the book. The design can be produced by many means and
techniques, including tooling in gold, silver, black and many different colours,
onlaying and inlaying coloured leathers and other materials, sculpting
the surface of the boards, and various painting and batik techniques. All these
materials and techniques provide more scope for expressive design than
are available to the artist who works on paper or canvas, and yet art on paper
and canvas still commands more attention and respect. The time must
come when it is recognized that bookbinding can provide first-class craftsmanship with integrated designs of almost limitless possibilities, either expressive or just brilliantly decorative.

The responsibility to preserve existing bindings and the works they cover
is as great as that to create new bindings. The need for conservation programs
is being increasingly recognized, but even so one fears that the allocation
of funds will be inadequate for years to come. In Britain the economic situation
provides an excuse which has partial validity, but one feels that in the
United States even more could be achieved than has already been accomplished
—immense sums are spent on prestigious acquisitions while current hold-

ings rot. If funding is not greatly increased many binders and restorers will continue to work alone or with one or two colleagues, and have to cope with too wide a range of problems, at the same time trying to keep pace with current research and development of improved materials. This is no easy task and the responsibility is heavy. Communications are today very good, seminars are frequent and technical literature is abundant, but very often there is no substitute for day-to-day consultation with colleagues as the work progresses. This is likely to remain a serious problem in the United States where distances are so great. As archival and library material deteriorates and problems increase, the selection of trainees with good brains and aptitude for productivity as distinct from leisurely craftsmanship will be of even greater importance than it is now. It will be important because the training period is long and the number of craftsmen who are competent to teach is so small that we cannot afford to have a high wastage rate of trainees, or to have 'passengers' working in the field.

There is also the silicon chip factor which we are assured will soon revolutionize industry and reduce working hours. No doubt many people who have

interesting work like conservators will be happy to work somewhat longer
hours than most, but it does seem quite likely that the working week will be
reduced in a few years' time, with serious consequences for output and the
care of libraries. The Hunt Institute for Botanical Documentation has
an exceptionally enlightened conservation policy, but overall, nationally and
internationally, one fears that in the absence of a huge effort cultural losses
will be disastrous.

During the past seventy years or so, the craft of bookbinding has evolved
to meet the needs of a changing market which itself has resulted from a
gradual restructuring of our social systems. That evolution will continue and
make considerable demands on those who practice this compelling craft,
which is never mastered in all its many facets by any one craftsman. Although
it is an ancient craft it still has considerable vitality both technically and
aesthetically, as this exhibition clearly demonstrates, and must surely have a
bright and immensely important future.

Bernard C. Middleton, January 25, 1979

The movement that later became known by the name Arts and Crafts
began as an attempt by a handful of English gentlemen to purge their country
of its appallingly tasteless furnishings and buildings, and to create a new sense
of beauty based upon utility and morality. It was a natural reaction to the
situation obtaining in English design at the middle of the nineteenth century,
but it came about with such vigour because conditions had significantly
worsened between 1860 and 1880. As William Morris, the leader of this
group, noted, life with all its modern mechanical achievements, comforts and
luxuries, was growing "uglier every day." But to properly understand the
ideals of the movement, one must first look at those aspects of the Industrial
Revolution that had been bringing about this decay in design standards
since the last decade of the eighteenth century.

Those miracles of modern invention that were bringing to England ever
increasing prosperity and material goods were also the cause of the rot setting
in. The new transport that made building materials cheaper than they had
ever been, and the machines that made possible a vastly increased production
of goods, gave rise to ugliness as well as the well-known Victorian exhilaration.
The making of things, whether buildings, crockery or clothing, had always
been governed by what materials were cheapest and by what was feasible in the
way of decoration. But now we had a situation where a house could
be built more cheaply from transported bricks than from local stone. Thanks to
machines, simple designs could be replaced by endless repetitive ornament;
and hand embroidery could not compete with machine-made lace. It has
been said that before the railways came there was not an ugly house in
England—unsanitary, overcrowded, or rundown perhaps, but still in harmony
with its surroundings. The tradition of craftsmen using local materials to
work out the best designs was now broken. Manufacturers were so enamored
of the exciting possibilities offered by machines that they used them to
excess. The Victorians littered their living rooms with spring-upholstered
furniture and senseless manufactured knick-knacks. But machine-made goods
and the breaking of local craft traditions were not the only causes of the
fall in design standards; another was the rise of a huge new middle class which
could afford to buy these goods—the uneducated rich, the self-made men.

Lastly, one must not forget that Victorians seemed actually to want a break in tradition. Quite apart from it being easier to build Gothic than in the past, they desired a revival of Gothic architecture and ornament.

The Arts and Crafts movement was concerned not only with things that were made, but also with the persons who made them. With the organization of industry on a grand scale, the producer, i.e., the designer and craftsman, was lost sight of. There was no longer an individual turning out an item as well as he might for a particular use in a particular household. Now there was a mass of workers turning out chairs or teapots or cloth as fast as they could for unknown buyers. Manufactured goods were often well made for the price, and they were decorated in a manner that would appeal to an anonymous buyer. Most households had risen above the level of poverty and could afford things that were not the bare necessities. Indeed, many could afford the best. But what was the best? Simply, it was the cheapest gilt. It was a simple design carried to extreme, in silk instead of linen. Given the circumstances, it was not surprising that sooner or later, persons with time, money and taste should come forward and try to put a stop to this trend. Nor should it have been surprising that they came from the upper-middle class rather than from skilled craftsmen or artisans, for most of these people had moved from their country villages or small workshops to be absorbed into factories in the industrial areas, and were not in a position to alter the methods or designs of their employers.

The rumblings of Thomas Carlyle on the "condition of England" led Ruskin to his pontifications on artistic standards and the superiority of the pre-Raphaelites and, in 1862, to his advocacy of socialism in *Unto this last*. Ruskin was the undisputed prophet of the movement, and believed that what was needed was a revival of design in handicraft, a uniting or reuniting of the artist and the craftsman. However it was with William Morris that the movement really got under way. Morris' initial interest upon arriving at Oxford in 1853 was in architecture (the Gothic revival architect Pugin had died the previous year), but under the influence of the painter Burne-Jones and other similar minds he soon turned to the tales, painting, interiors, and later, books, associated with the Gothic period. With Burne-Jones, Rossetti, Madox Brown, Philip Webb, Marshall and Faulkner, Morris set up a firm in 1861 producing stained glass and other items for churches. Later they branched out into wallpapers, domestic furniture, carpets and tapestries. As the business acquired notoriety, more men were employed and the movement gained momentum. Their work created a stir in artistic circles and was in great demand from churches and the upper classes who wanted something better than that available to the noveau-riche. But they felt that theirs was not just a movement destined to produce fine furnishings for the rich.

It was also a protest against the industrial progress that produced shoddy
wares, the cheapness of which was paid for by men's lives. A man who worked
6 days a week from 6 to 9 was no more than a machine himself. Moreover, they asserted that the practice of handicrafts was good for the individual.
Whether he be a professional man trying his hand at bookbinding,
or a working man doing woodcarving on his day off, he would be fulfilling a
common and primitive urge and would delight in ordinary things made
beautiful. Thus Art as Crafts was the great socializer. It made the rich man
humble by forcing him to work with his hands, and the humble man
rich by producing a thing of beauty.

The movement became yet more widely known through the Arts and
Crafts Exhibition Society. It was their exhibitions and the lectures that accom-
panied them which showed the world that there was indeed an awakened
feeling for beauty in the accessories of life, and moreover that there
were persons who could produce such articles. Since 1858, when Madox
Brown had tried to exhibit his designs for furniture at the Hogarth
Club and had been refused on the grounds that they were not "art proper," the
designer-craftsman had been handicapped by having nowhere to exhibit.
Morris felt that his company's wares could be seen in his shop window and did
not need exhibitions as did paintings. But others in the group disagreed.
In 1884 a loose association was formed under the name of the Art Workers'
Guild, and it was from among the members of this Guild that the idea
of an Arts and Crafts Exhibition Society was formed. The Society consisted
of about twenty-five men brought together by W. A. S. Benson and
included T. J. Cobden-Sanderson who suggested the name. Their idea was to
put on display the best in design and craft so that others might know what
to strive for. Groups of artists and craftsmen had been springing up all
around the country under the influence of Ruskin, but they had no standards
of quality and perhaps did as much harm as good to the movement. The
organizers of the Society each contributed ideas about the way the designer-
craftsman should work and these had a great influence on the next generation.
Not the least of these principles was that propounded by Cobden-Sanderson,
that the names of designer and craftsman should be published as joint
authors of a piece of work. It was unheard of for a firm to name the man who
designed something in their workshops, let alone the man who actually
carried out the work. Morris himself took a cool view of naming the "responsible executant" of his own designs, feeling that it was the designer, not the
workmen, who was really responsible for the final results. As this was
essentially a designers' movement, it is not surprising that there was some
opposition.

The first Arts and Crafts Exhibition took place at the New Gallery in
London in the Autumn of 1888, and they continued annually, later triannually,

until after the turn of the century. But it was the early ones which had
most impact, as they marked the period of change. The catalogues of these first
exhibitions contain notes by the various members in the Society, who
wrote not in a literary style but as actual designers and workmen, on the
subjects of the exhibits: textiles, decorative painting, wallpapers, fictiles
(pottery), metal work, stone and wood carving, furniture, stained glass, printing and bookbinding. Another contribution by Cobden-Sanderson to
the success of these exhibitions was his proposal of a series of lectures to accompany them. He believed that it was not enough to do good work, but
that one's work must be progressive and living. In order for it to be so, one
must be able to express one's views by word of mouth in a logical fashion for
others to hear. Not unlike the seminars which are to accompany this
exhibition at the Hunt Institute, these first lectures by men such as Morris,
Walter Crane, first president of the Society, Lethaby and Cobden-Sanderson
probably had more effect on the practising craftsmen than the exhibitions
themselves. In addition to his lectures, Cobden-Sanderson showed at the first
exhibition about twenty books; according to his principles, these were
listed as sewn by his wife Annie, "edges gilt by Gwyn, designed, forwarded,
gauffered and finished" by himself. At the 1889 exhibition he had another
twenty books. This was his period of greatest productivity as a bookbinder.

Cobden-Sanderson did for bookbinding what Morris and Company had
done for textiles and furnishings. He turned it upside down, revolutionizing
the way the binder approaches his craft. He was, in fact, the first modern
bookbinder. By this I do not mean that he chose to be modern—far from it—
but that all twentieth-century bookbinding has followed the ideals and
principles set forth by him. Born Thomas James Sanderson in 1840 (he added
his wife's name to his own on marriage), he did not take up bookbinding
until 1883 when he decided he did not have the temperament for the legal
career into which he had fallen after leaving Cambridge without a degree.
He met Morris and Burne-Jones and their circle in the 1860s, when he was
amused by their "medievalism." He was interested in their socialist ideas and
was looking for a handicraft which he might practice while leaving his
mind free for reflection—which he had always considered his most important
occupation. When Mrs. Morris noted that their circle did not have a bookbinder, Cobden-Sanderson leapt at the idea. He remembered how he had
often told the binder de Coverley, when taking him a book, "I shall one day
come to you, and ask you to make me a bookbinder." And so he did, first
having a few lessons in his rooms, then going into the workshop to
learn properly. He learned sewing and forwarding, and even at this stage
de Coverley noted that he "was always trying to find out the best way of doing
things and would take no end of pains with the most simple job." No wonder
he was laughed at by the bindery workmen for his quaint ideas. They were

not prepared for a bookbinder who could think for himself. They were used to
turning out bindings as a factory turned out shirts—as cheaply as possible.
The price offered determined the time spent on a book and the materials and
methods used, and as trade competition was fierce, no book could be
refused. It was not up to the binder to use his own judgement about the quality
of leather, the type of sewing or the style of decoration. The finish was
more or less elaborate, always following the traditional patterns used in the
past, according to the price to be paid. It was out of the question for a
binder to consider reading the book before he set to bind it, even if he could
read. De Coverley's, like Riviere, Morrell and Zaehnsdorf, was producing fine and expensive bindings in the 1880s but never original designs.
Bookbinders were far more interested in the niceties of perfect finishing
and the extremes to which traditional designs could be carried than with
creating something new. They had become machines of the Industrial
Revolution without even becoming mechanized. No wonder Morris thought
bookbinding was an unnecessary craft and could perhaps be better done
by machine.

When Cobden-Sanderson left de Coverley after some months, he set up
on his own to practice finishing. Such was his success that by November 1885
de Coverley remarked that he need not fear comparison with any finisher
in London. In 1886 he began selling his bindings through the bookseller
Bain, and soon his books were in great demand, fetching prices the trade
binders never dreamed possible. After the Arts and Crafts Exhibitions of 1888
and 1889, and his lectures and interviews, there was even more demand for
his books in England and America. In 1893 he set up the Doves Bindery with a
forwarder, finisher and sewer, all formerly from the staff of Riviere's. He
stopped binding books himself, but did all of the designs and supervised all the
work. Here he was able to fulfill what he saw to be the aims of the Arts
and Crafts movement. As when he worked alone, there were to be no false
economies; that is, no artificial raised bands, no dishonest materials such
as artificially grained leather, and no patterned rolls to speed up the finishing.
His was a happy group, working reasonable hours for reasonable pay
(unlike the men working for Morris, the staff of the Doves earned well above
what they could get elsewhere) with paid holidays and time for discussion
of the books they were binding. Above all they agreed on the standards and
ideals of design, materials and craftsmanship, and worked as a unit toward
that end. Cobden-Sanderson, not the market, set the price of a Doves binding.

In his reflections Cobden-Sanderson worked out what he called a "vision"
or ideal towards which man or society should strive. His vision of the world
and society within it is perhaps cast far in the future, but his vision of the
bookbinder was really a perfected image of himself: a man both artist and

craftsman, intelligent and sensitive to the beauty of literature and printing, with
the time and freedom to practice his craft as it should be. The utmost aim
of the binder should be perfection and appropriateness, seeking the best possible
materials and tools without regard to price, and using the soundest methods
of binding without regard to time. Cobden-Sanderson, like Morris,
felt that the best work is done when there is a union of the higher work with
the lower, the mind with the hand. He was proud of making his own
paste, doing his own sewing, and when necessary, gilding his own edges. However he was not under the impression that ideal conditions of work could
produce good work. Good original designs came as the result of imagina-
tive genius and could not be taught. But when elaborate binding was
not called for, he agreed with his fellow craftsmen in the movement that plain
work skillfully executed, using carefully selected honest materials, had
beauty far superior to the "deplorable miracles of misapplied skill" which
one so often saw.

What Cobden-Sanderson brought to bookbinding and to the Arts and
Crafts movement was more than its name. It was his forward vision, and his

flexible and experimental approach to the craft that made him stand out
from the essentially backward-looking medieval thinking of Morris and others
in the movement. Although his books tend to look much like one another,
a close, chronological inspection shows that there are gradual changes in
his methods and materials. He discarded one thing for another which proved
superior for the purpose, even abandoning treasured methods such as
tight back and raised cords when a hollow back was warranted. For although
Cobden-Sanderson was a prime mover in the Arts and Crafts movement
and was only a few years younger than Morris, his approach to bookbinding was essentially scientific. He was more of a twentieth century man
than a Victorian. His hero was Alexander von Humboldt, not the prede-
cessors of Raphael. However his aim was that of Ruskin and Morris: "to dignify
labour in all the lower crafts; to induce men of education to follow in
the same direction, and so to lift all the arts and crafts, upon which life rests,
by the spirit in which they are performed; to consecrate the arts and
crafts to the well-being of society as a whole."

Marianne Fletcher Titcombe, February 1979

23

Beginning with its founder, Rachel McMasters Miller Hunt, and continuing through Thomas W. Patterson and Jean Gunner, the Hunt Institute has participated in the tradition of fine binding. An early encounter with T. J. Cobden-Sanderson's philosophy of bookbinding as a craft that aimed at "pleasure in the intelligent work of the hand, and honor in the formation and maintenance of a great and historic tradition"[1] had a lasting effect on the young Miss Miller. Her understanding of these ideals of craftsmanship was evidenced both in her own work in bookbinding and in her later collecting of books for their contents and coverings. Her botanical collection, now grown into the Hunt Botanical Library at the Institute, is one in which both beauty and utility must be conserved. Curators and binders have cooperated to maintain the books in working order, enhancing their physical well-being while preserving their bibliographical integrity.

[1]Cobden-Sanderson, *"Bookbinding,"* p. 325.

I. RACHEL MCMASTERS MILLER HUNT *1909*

Alfred Lord Tennyson. *Seven poems and two translations*. Hammersmith, the Doves Press, 1902.

Green crushed levant morocco, red morocco onlays, gold tooling. Cloudy green and purple endpapers, rose levant doublures, gold-tooled; rough gilt edges. Double green silk endbands; projecting endcaps, five raised bands. 233 x 167 mm. Signed: RMcMM 19 [lamb] 09

Rachel McMasters Miller Hunt (1882-1963) was a bookbinder in the Cobden-Sanderson tradition and was greatly influenced by his ideals of high quality materials and honest technique. Inspired to learn bookbinding after an early visit to the Roycrofters, she studied under Euphemia Bakewell. Meeting T. J. Cobden-Sanderson in 1907, she maintained a correspondence with him and his daughter Stella, whom she visited frequently. Mrs. Hunt therefore typified the many early twentieth century binders of whom Sarah Prideaux has said, "In America there is hardly a centre where there is any interest shown in books which has not a woman binder who has probably been trained by Mr. Cobden-Sanderson." Mrs. Hunt exhibited her

bindings widely, including in the first annual exhibition of the Guild of
Book Workers in 1907. Her last binding, on an eighteenth century English
gardening book, was begun on 14 April 1920. This work, never completed,
is shelved with similar works in the Hunt Botanical Library and links
her lifelong interests of fine binding and botanical books and gardening. She
continued to write and lecture on bookbinding and gave her finishing
tools and equipment in 1961 to the bindery established at the Hunt Botanical
Library.

REFERENCES: Titcombe, *Bookbinding career*, no. 40. Prideaux, *Modern
bookbindings*, p. 53.

Hunt Botanical Library

2. RACHEL MCMASTERS MILLER HUNT   *1911*

Francis Bacon and Abraham Cowley. *On gardens.* London, the Astolat
Press, 1903.

Bright green crushed levant morocco, red onlays, gold tooling. Japanese
scenery endpapers; gilt edges. Single green silk endbands; five raised bands.
173 x 110 mm. Signed: RMcMM ∴ 1911.

REFERENCE: Titcombe, *Bookbinding career*, no. 63.

Hunt Botanical Library

3. THOMAS W. PATTERSON   *1964*

Roger Heim and Robert Wasson. *Les champignons hallucinogènes du Mexique.*
Paris, Editions du Muséum National d'Histoire Naturelle, 1958.

Black oasis morocco, white pigskin and terra cotta oasis inlays, gold tooling.
Green, charcoal and orange striped ecru endpapers and doublures.
Double white, green, red and gold endbands; smooth spine. 327 x 252 mm.
Signed: 19 TWP [monogram] 64

Thomas W. Patterson (1905-1972), Master Binder at the Hunt Institute
from 1961 until his death, had been acquainted with Mrs. Hunt and her
collections since the early 1930s. His formal training consisted of several courses

at the Carnegie Institute of Technology, supplemented by reading, experimentation and practice. He was an active member of the Guild of
Book Workers for more than 35 years, and was its vice-president at large from
1960-65. Much of his later work at the Hunt Institute involved restoration
and conservation of the Institute's collections.

REFERENCE: *Thomas W. Patterson, bookbinder*, no. 49.

Hunt Botanical Library

4. JEAN GUNNER *1978-1979* 27

Crispijn Van de Passe. *Hortus floridus*. London, Cresset Press, 1928-1929.
Two volumes.

Volume I. Brilliant green oasis morocco, shades of red, yellow and green
oasis inlays and onlays, gold and blind tooling. Yellow dyed Japanese paper
endpapers and red dyed Japanese paper doublures; top edge gilt. Single
light and dark red silk endbands; smooth spine. 172 x 242 mm. Signed:
J. Gunner 1978

Volume II. Brilliant green oasis morocco, shades of purple, blue, yellow,
green and natural oasis inlays and onlays, gold and blind tooling. Purple dyed
Japanese paper endpapers and yellow dyed Japanese paper doublures; top
edge gilt. Single purple, white and blue silk endbands; smooth spine.
172 x 242 mm. Signed: J. Gunner 1978

Jean Gunner, born in 1947, received her early training in bookbinding
and related subjects at the Epsom and Ewell School of Art and Crafts and the
Guildford School of Art from 1962-1967. Coming to the United States
in 1969, she worked for and studied restoration under Carolyn Horton. After
working briefly at the newly established conservation department at the
New York Public Library, she came to the Hunt Institute in 1972. She has
taken courses at the Institute of Paper Chemistry and the India Office
paper conservation department. Particularly interested in the teaching of
bookbinding, she has taught private classes in boxmaking, bookbinding and
repair since 1973, and has recently begun teaching in the design department
of Carnegie-Mellon University. She has also lectured and written articles on
binding and conservation.

Hunt Botanical Library

1. *Rachel McMasters Miller Hunt, 1909*

2. *Rachel McMasters Miller Hunt, 1911*

3. *Thomas W. Patterson, 1964*

32

4a. *Jean Gunner, 1978*

4b. *Jean Gunner, 1978*

The Hunt Institute for Botanical Documentation includes a research library with books dating from the fifteenth century to the present. In order to keep these books in usable condition, the Institute operates a Bindery and Conservation Department where the main function is the boxing, repair, and rebinding of books. In determining which procedure to follow with a certain book, deterioration of paper, sewing, cloth and leather must be considered. When the original structure and covers of the book must be saved to preserve bibliographic integrity, the book is boxed to retard further deterioration. In repair, the original structure and cover of the book are retained where possible, and missing or damaged areas are replaced with new materials. In the event that the book has deteriorated beyond the point of repair, it is often partially or completely rebound. When the extent of deterioration has been determined, an outline for repair or rebinding can be formulated. This outline should include the techniques to be used in the underlying structure, materials to be used, and the decoration of the covers.

Focusing on the rebinding in full leather of books dating from the sixteenth century to the present, an aspect of this exhibition, I will concern myself here with the major operations pertaining to such work at the Hunt Institute. The methods described have been chosen to suit our needs and are not the only ones available to the bookbinder and restorer.

COLLATION
Upon receipt of the book, the original condition is noted, and a photograph may also be taken. Notes on pagination of the text block are important if the book is to be pulled for deacidification and resewing. Unidentified leaves and plates are collated and marked lightly with a pencil on an inner corner. Also at this time original labels, bookplates and other important bibliographic evidence are removed and preserved for inclusion after the book has been rebound.

POLLUTION
Since the start of industrial pollution in the early nineteenth century, many materials have been exposed to a variety of contaminants. Sulphur dioxide, one of the main pollutants, is often absorbed into paper, forming sulphurous

and sulphuric acid. In such cases the acid stains and embrittles paper, causing extensive damage. Where possible, a book which has been subjected to such pollution is carefully collated, pulled, dry cleaned using special erasers which will not abrade the surface, and then deacidified.

IMAGE FIXING

Before proceeding with deacidification, inks are tested for stability. In the event that they are unstable, they are fixed with a mixture of gelatine and formaldehyde. As deacidification often changes any colored work, these leaves are treated by spraying deacidifying solution on the back of the work.

WASHING AND DEACIDIFICATION

Although there are non-aqueous deacidifying solutions available, we feel they need further scientific analysis before we can feel confident in using them. Where possible, we use an aqueous deacidifying process. After the book has been pulled, each conjugate leaf is interleaved with a wet-strength material for support. This is necessary because paper becomes very fragile when wet. The leaves are individually immersed and allowed to soak in running water until the water appears to be clear. Then, they are carefully transferred to a final bath of magnesium bicarbonate. This neutralizes any acids left in the paper, and also adds a buffer to ward off further attack by pollutants. When needed, a methyl cellulose sizing is added to the final bath to give the paper extra strength. The leaves are partially air dried on racks, and are then placed between blotting papers and put under a light weight until completely dry.

BLEACHING

Most of the discoloration in paper is removed during deacidification and, unless an unsightly stain is left, nothing more is done. Bleach is rarely used because imperfections are part of the history of the book and are left as such. Bleaching agents, themselves, are very controversial and can do extreme damage. Bleach cannot be completely washed out and, unless neutralized, can continue to bleach the paper and anything that comes into contact with it. When an unsightly or damaging stain must be removed, a mild solution of chloromine-T is used. The material is first deacidified, then bleached and then treated with an antichlor of sodium thiosulphate to neutralize the bleach. After washing thoroughly, it is again deacidified.

PAPER REPAIRS

When a book has been pulled, quite often the folds are weakened. These are repaired with narrow strips of Japanese tissue, affixed with a rice starch paste. Also at this time any tears or other major paper flaws are repaired. It is important that the original character of the paper not be destroyed during the repair process. Repair papers and tissues are selected to harmonize with the original. The character of the paper and extent of damage to

each individual text block determines the repair method to be used. Basically
we use two methods: long fiber (using Japanese paper) and inlays (using
matching papers). The long fiber is used for extensive damage and inlays where
there is less damage. Paper repairs can be one of the most time-consuming
processes in binding. The technique chosen must be reversible, as with
all processes in bookbinding and repair.

SEWING

Once the paper repairs have been completed, the leaves are collated back into
their original signature form and the book is readied for sewing. The
technique chosen for sewing is one of the most important decisions in the
binding of a book, for it helps determine how well the book will open.
The size of the book, flexibility of the paper and the width of the inner margin
are all major factors in the sewing decision. When we resew a rare book,
we always incorporate a continuous guard. This is a piece of thin handmade
paper or Japanese tissue cut to the length of the book and folded into accordion
pleats. In sewing, each signature is placed into an individual pleat. This
method creates a very flexible binding allowing the leaves to lie flat more easily
when the book is open. Also, as modern bookbinding adhesives are
difficult to remove, the continuous guard prevents the adhesive from coming
into contact with the text block.

When a smooth spine is desired, we take pieces of pure unbleached linen
cord and flatten out the portions that are to cover the spine. We use cords
rather than tapes, as we prefer to lace them rather than tapes into the boards.
A herringbone stitch is used when sewing around the flattened cords. This
helps keep the tension of the sewing even throughout and reduces the amount
of swelling at the spine caused by the continuous guard. Pure unbleached
linen cord is also used when raised cords are desired. When sewing around the
cords, the thread is wrapped around a few extra times to equal the thickness
of the signature. This is called "arch sewing," and helps compact the spine
as well as making a very flexible binding.

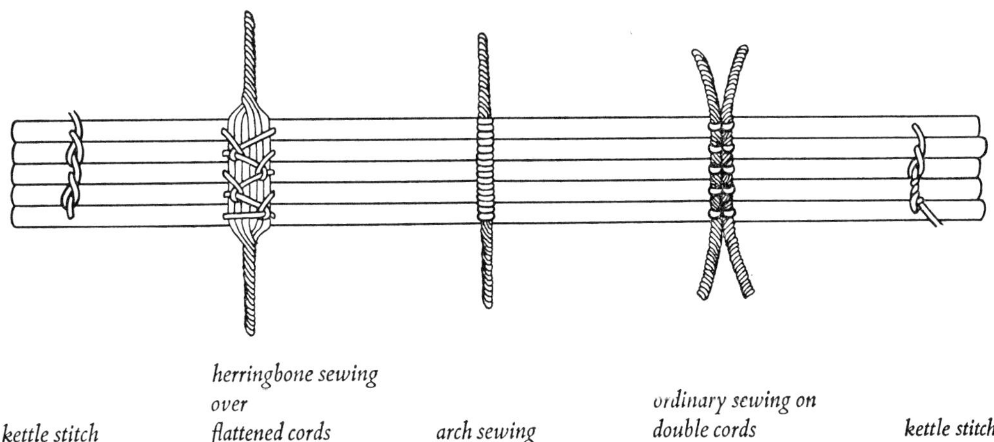

FLYLEAVES AND ENDPAPERS

The flyleaves are the plain leaves that lead into the text block at the front and back of the book. If it is necessary to use new flyleaves, they are selected to harmonize with the character and color of the text block. The endpaper is the fold of marbled, printed, colored or plain paper that you usually see upon opening the book, part of which becomes the board pastedown. Selection of the endpapers is important. The design and colors should have the feeling of the time in which the book was printed. There are many ways of making up and reinforcing endpapers, but whatever method we decide to use, we always reinforce the folds with pure linen cloth. The linen serves a dual purpose: it strengthens the flyleaf and also the hinge of the book as it overlaps onto the boards. The endpapers are then sewn on, using the same methods as for the text block.

GLUING UP THE SPINE

Placed between binder's boards, the book is jogged up on the head and spine to align the signatures, and then put into a press. When the sewing techniques previously described are used, only a light coat of glue (synthetic resin) on the spine is necessary.

EDGE TRIMMING

On modern books where a gilded edge is preferred, the edges may be trimmed, removing a minimum amount of paper. Under no circumstances are early or other valuable materials trimmed. The trimming of such materials has sometimes been done to neaten the edges after resewing. However, in doing this the original character of the book is changed, often destroying important bibliographic evidence which may be of value to later scholars.

ROUNDING AND BACKING

When the glued spine is almost dry, the book is removed from the press and boards. The spine is then rounded. Except on our old and rare books, the book is put between backing boards and placed in a press under heavy pressure and the shoulders are formed by using a hammer. As this process can further weaken already weak paper or stiffen the spine considerably when the paper is heavy stock, we prefer to eliminate the backing process in such cases. Instead, we bevel the inside edges of the cover boards to accommodate the swelling in the spine. We have found that by using this technique, the book will lie quite flat when opened, and keep its shape without any problems.

BOARDS AND THEIR ATTACHMENT

After the boards have been cut to size, they are lined with acid-free paper as binder's board often contains acids. This also helps prevent excessive warping when the leather cover is put on. The boards are then beveled at the spine edge, as previously described. The outside edges are gently beveled using sandpaper, the fore-edge corners gently rounded, and the inside edges are sanded smooth.

The cords of the book are laced into the boards through holes punched at the spine edge. Preceding the lacing-in, grooves are cut into the boards to receive the overlapping cords, which are pasted into position after the endbands have been sewn on.

ENDBANDS

Endbands are not merely decorative, but structurally important as reinforcements for the ends of the spine if sewn directly onto the text block. We tie them down at each signature to ensure maximum strength. There are many styles of endbanding, using either cotton, linen or silk thread, with the date and place of publication of the book determining the type to be used.

SPINE LININGS

Spine linings can play a major role in determining how well a book will open. If heavy and stiff linings are used, force often will be required to open the book, eventually causing damage to the binding structure. If the spine is smooth, we line it from head to tail, including the endbands, with acid-free paper. The endband area is then lined with leather. When there are raised cords, strips of acid-free paper are glued on between the cords, again with leather over the endband area. In both cases, when there are beveled boards, the lining is overlapped onto the boards. Because there is no shoulder to hold the boards in place, this overlapping is done to prevent the boards from rising up when the book is covered in. When the linings have dried, they are sanded until smooth.

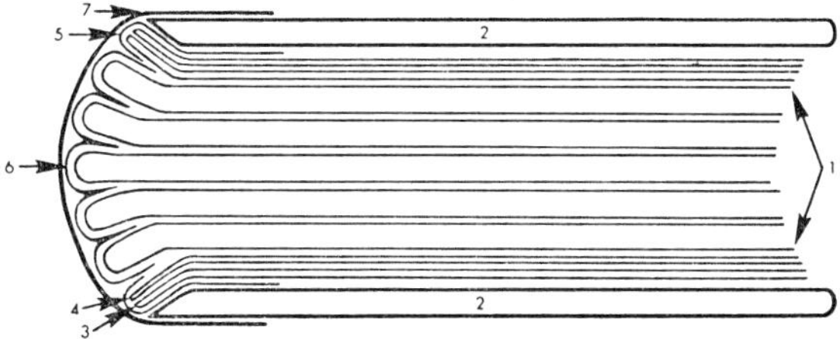

1. *text block*
2. *beveled cover boards*
3. *endpapers*
4. *flyleaves*
5. *reinforcing linen hinge*
6. *continuous guard*
7. *spine lining overlapped onto boards*

COVERING

The text block is capped-up, i.e., wrapped with paper to protect the text block, while the book is covered in. We commonly use goat and calf skins, which are cut to size and pared at the turn-ins and slightly in the spine and hinge area. The leather is then dampened on the hair side, pasted, and the book covered in. After the leather has dried the turn-ins are trimmed, leaving an even border of leather around the inside of the boards. The linen hinges are then glued into place. Depending on the thickness of the

leather, lightweight board is cut and glued onto the inside of the boards,
"filling in" the area not covered with leather.

DESIGN

For any of our valuable older books, we prefer a design that has a feeling
of the book's period. Where twentieth century books are concerned, we are
free to use our artistic freedom, and it is here that one's own characteristic
styles are developed.

Designing the cover of a book takes many hours. Sketches are made and
remade before the final design is selected. This design must then be worked
out precisely to fit the dimensions of the book and a pattern may be made
to work from.

INLAYS

When colored areas are desired, inlays or onlays are used. Generally inlays
are used for the larger areas of the design that are to be a different color from
the cover leather. The shape is cut out of thin board, saving the outer frame.
Using clear tape, the shape is taped around the edges onto the chosen piece
of leather. The leather shape is then cut out beveling towards the center. The
outer frame is taped into position onto the book, and the cover leather
is cut out, again beveling towards the center. The inlay is then pasted into
position, making sure that the beveled edges are butted together.

ONLAYS

The leather used in onlays is pared very thin and the desired shapes are cut
out of thin board. The shapes are then pasted onto the leather. When dry, the
leather is cut out around the shapes. They are then pasted, put in position
on the book and pressed into the cover. After they have dried, the board is
carefully removed, leaving the "onlaid" leather in position.

BLIND TOOLING

The paper pattern for the tooling is taped to the book. With heated tools a
"blind" impression is made on the leather using the pattern as a guide.
The pattern is then removed and the impressions are dampened with water.
The heated tool is again pressed into the impression. The darkness of the design
is determined by the degree of dampness and the temperature of the tool.

GOLD TOOLING

For gold tooling, the previous steps are followed but without the application of water. Instead, the impressions are prepared with two coats of glaire.

The choice of glaire is purely personal; there are organic ones made with
egg whites as well as synthetic shellac glaires. We prefer to use the latter. Glaire
is necessary to make the gold leaf adhere in the impressions. After the
glaire has dried, two layers of gold leaf are applied over the impressions.
With the heated tool, the gold is carefully pressed into the original impression. The excess gold is then removed with a gold eraser.

FINAL PROCESSES
After the design is completed, the covers, spine, edges and turn-ins are
polished using a heated polishing iron. This can be done several times with
the iron hotter each time until the desired degree of luster is obtained.
This process makes the grain of the leather very pronounced and adds a glow
to the colors. It is not done when a dull finish is required.

The final step is the pasting-down of the board papers. They are trimmed so
that an even border of leather is showing on the three edges, then pasted
into position. As soon as the hinge area of the board paper is dry, the boards are
closed onto the book and it is placed under a weight for at least twenty-four
hours, although preferably for several days.

It is our policy at the Institute to make a drop-back felt-lined box for all
new full leather bindings. This protects the books from fading and the hazards
of open shelving, such as scratches and dust.

CONCLUSION
The design processes described are just four methods commonly used
at the Hunt Institute. Materials such as palladium leaf, colored foils, plastics,
jewels, fabrics, and woods could be used to embellish a book cover. As
with any works of art in the twentieth century, there seems to be no limitation
on designs or materials used. Amidst all these possibilities it is my hope
for the craft and art of bookbinding that the integrity of the book not be lost,
a challenge to the creative bookbinder which should not be forgotten.

ACKNOWLEDGEMENTS
I am especially indebted to Mr. Bernard C. Middleton for his guidance
on technical matters, to Mrs. Marianne Titcombe for constructive suggestions
and to Mrs. Olivia Primanis Cherin for her patience and assistance in
getting me started on this article.

Jean Gunner, 1979

(See Hunt Binders, page 25, for entries 1 through 4.)

BLIND-STAMPED AND BLIND-TOOLED BINDINGS

In the history of binding ornamentation, blind stamping the leather with metal or wooden tools was one of the earliest techniques and is one that has survived to the present day. Variations on the panel stamp, a consolidation of several designs, usually including a pictorial center, occur occasionally in modern fine binding. Blind stamping in patterns reminiscent of earlier styles can be an effective modern technique, recalling, for example, the elaborate Romanesque bindings of the twelfth century or the multiply bordered German bindings of the fifteenth and sixteenth centuries. In the modern idiom, blind tooling can be used to achieve a subtle play of textures and shadows, or, in combination with gold tooling, to enhance the richness of the gold.

5. BLIND-TOOLED BINDING WITH PANEL STAMP
ca. 1574

Otto Brunfels. *Herbarum vivae eicones.* Strassburg, J. Schott, 1532-1539.

White pigskin, blind-tooled and -stamped. Plain endpapers; sprinkled blue edges. Single natural linen endbands; four raised bands. Metal corners and clasps. 336 x 225 mm.

The concentric rectangular borders include an unsigned portrait roll of the reformers, labeled Johannes Huss, Philip Melan, Erasmus Rote, Martinus Luth. The front cover has a panel stamp showing the crucifixion and is signed MV. The panel stamp on the back cover is a portrait of Philip Melanchthon, and is signed HB. The sixteenth century monogramists MV and HB, whose panel stamps are frequently found together, were probably engravers rather than bookbinders. The initials BOH and the date 1574 on the front cover probably refer to an early owner.

REFERENCES: *Hunt catalogue,* no. 30. Haebler, *Rollen- und Plattenstempel,* vol. 1, pp. 49-50, 464-469; vol. 2, p. 203. Text accompanying crucifixion stamp varies from that noted in Haebler, no. 20, reading: Sanguis · Ihesu · Chriti · filii · dei · / emundat · nos · ab · omni · peccato.

Hunt Botanical Library, from the original collection of Rachel McMasters Miller Hunt

6. DOVES BINDERY
1897

Geoffrey Chaucer. *The works of Geoffrey Chaucer.* Hammersmith, Kelmscott Press, 1896.

White pigskin, blind-tooled and -stamped. Plain endpapers; rough gilt edges. Single green silk endbands; projecting endcaps, four raised bands; silver clasps. 438 x 287 mm. Signed: The Doves Bindery   1897

Based on designs by William Morris, this binding was tooled, mainly by Douglas Cockerell, under the supervision of T. J. Cobden-Sanderson at the Doves Bindery. The design of vine leaves is similar to the intertwined woodcut borders in the text itself, also designed by Morris.

Approximately 48 copies of this work were bound using this same design over a period of at least four years. Several variants exist. The binding dated 1900, illustrated in the Brown University Library catalogue, lacks the square floral tools on either side of the word Kelmscott. This may have been tooled by Charles McLeish after Cockerell left the Bindery in 1898. Cobden-Sanderson also designed another pigskin binding for the *Chaucer,* extensively gold-tooled, with vines, leaves and a pointilliste center, bordered with the opening lines of the Canterbury Tales.

REFERENCES: Miner, *History of bookbinding,* no. 571. Needham, *William Morris,* no. 100. Brown University Library, *William Morris,* pl. XV. Hobson, G. D., *English bindings,* no. 119.

George Peabody Department, Enoch Pratt Free Library

7. BLIND-TOOLED QUARTER PIGSKIN BINDING
ca. 1896-1921

Geoffrey Chaucer. *The works of Geoffrey Chaucer.* Hammersmith, Kelmscott Press, 1896.

Oak boards, quarter pigskin, blind-tooled. Plain endpapers. Single beige silk endbands; projecting endcaps, five double raised bands. 440 x 310 mm.

Although the tools used in this unsigned binding are not those used in the full pigskin bindings done for the Kelmscott *Chaucer* by the Doves Bindery, it could be Doves Bindery work. In an interview published in the *Daily Chronicle,* August 8, 1896, S. C. Cockerell spoke of "Another copy [of the *Chaucer*] we have bound in half-pigskin with oak boards, a style which was very common in the middle ages, but the mediaeval bookbinders more frequently used beech than oak." The broad oak foliage tooled in relief is similar to that designed by William Morris for the lower cover of the full pigskin binding.

If this binding, of which there are several copies known, was done at the Doves Bindery, the tooling was probably done by Charles McLeish. Although he had left his position as finisher there in 1909, all bindings signed "Doves Bindery" and completed between 1909 and 1921 were bound in the McLeish workshop.

REFERENCE: Maggs, *Catalogue 966,* no. 247.

Private collection

8. DON ETHERINGTON   *1977*

Geoffrey Chaucer. *The works of Geoffrey Chaucer.* Hammersmith, Kelmscott Press, 1896.

White alum-tawed pigskin, blind- and gold-tooled. White alum-tawed doublures. Blue and white chevron-patterned endbands; five raised bands. 422 x 297 mm. Signed: Don Etherington

The tooling is reminiscent of the text's printed borders.

Don Etherington, born in 1935, received his early training at the Central School of Arts and Crafts in London and worked in the bindery of Roger Powell and Peter Waters. He has taught bookbinding at the Camberwell and Southampton Colleges of Art. Coming to the Library of Congress, he began as Training Officer in the Library's preservation program. He is now the Assistant Restoration Officer and is particularly responsible for the development and subsequent publication of improved techniques in conservation.

REFERENCE: *Hand bookbinding today,* no. 24.

Rare Book and Special Collections Division, Library of Congress, Washington, D.C.

9. BLIND-STAMPED BINDING   *ca. early 20th century*

Rembert Dodoens. *Stirpium historiae pemptades sex.* Antwerp, Christopher Plantin, 1583.

Tan polished calf, tooled and stamped in blind. Marbled endpapers; orange stained edges. Single cream and tan silk endbands; five raised bands. 353 x 220 mm.

The Hunt Botanical Library includes a number of sixteenth century herbals from the collection of F. W. T. Hunger (1874-1952), a botanical author and book collector. This one and the others may have been rebound to match original sixteenth century bindings in his collection.

PROVENANCE: Bookplate of F. W. T. Hunger.

REFERENCE: *Hunt catalogue,* no. 143.

Hunt Botanical Library, from the original collection of Rachel McMasters Miller Hunt

10. CAROLYN HORTON & ASSOCIATES   *1977*

Bartholomaeus Anglicus. *De proprietatibus rerum.* Nuremberg, Anton Koberger, 1492.

Dark brown calf, blind-tooled. Plain endpapers; uncut edges. Single natural linen endbands; three double raised bands. Original bronze center bosses, corners and clasps. 316 x 227 mm. Signed: Horton Bindery Binder's ticket: Carolyn Horton & Associates

Badly damaged in the Corning flood in 1972, this work was rebound in the "Koberger" or Nuremberg style of the late fifteenth century, reusing the original boards, ornaments and clasps. The remains of the original binding accompany the new work.

Carolyn Horton, born in 1909, received her early training in Vienna at the Frauen Akadamie für angewandten Kunst. She was apprenticed to Albert Oldach & Son in Philadelphia before setting up her first studio there in 1934. From 1935 to 1939 she did restoration work for the American Philosophical Society's library and worked in a similar capacity for the Yale University Library from 1939 to

1941. Before establishing her present studio in New York City in 1958, she did extensive free-lance work for libraries in Washington, Chicago and New York. Starting with two small rooms, her studio has expanded into four levels of a five story house where books, documents and works of art on paper are preserved by staff under her direction. She has written and lectured widely on her experiences as a conservator, particularly those in the wake of such library disasters as the floods in Florence and Corning. Her book, *Cleaning and preserving bindings and related materials,* first published in 1967, is a standard manual for simple preventive measures and library repairs.

REFERENCE: Miner, *History of bookbinding,* p. 69.

Corning Museum of Glass

11. FRITZ EBERHARDT   *1956*

Felix Timmermans. *Pieter Bruegel.* Wiesbaden, Insel Verlag, 1950.

Brown oasis, blind-tooled. Ivory endpapers; top edge gilt. Single golden yellow silk endbands; seven raised bands. 200 x 124 mm.

The binding is shown with the four woodblock tools cut by the binder and six drawings illustrating the development of the design.

Born in Silesia in 1917, Fritz Eberhardt studied under binder Ignatz Wiemeler and calligrapher Rudo Spemann in Leipzig. Under the direction of Otto Fratzscher in Offenbach he received his diploma as a master bookbinder. In 1954 he and his wife, Trudi, also a bookbinder, came to the United States, where he began restoration work at the Library Company of Philadelphia. In 1956 the Eberhardts established their studio in Philadelphia. Eberhardt is known for his calligraphy as well as his hand-cut tools.

REFERENCE: Thompson, "Fritz Eberhardt, American binder."

Fritz Eberhardt; drawings and tools lent by binder.

VELLUM BINDINGS

More commonly considered a medium for fine manuscripts and early printing, vellum has also served as a binding material. Although vellum bindings have been intended as temporary in many cases, both limp and stiff types have been used by several fine and private presses, notably the Kelmscott Press. This use of vellum was an aspect of the medieval aesthetic that William Morris adhered to at first in the bindings for his "little typographical adventure," which culminated however in the great tooled pigskin bindings for the Kelmscott Chaucer. The structure and suitability of non-adhesive limp vellum bindings has been much studied in recent years by Christopher Clarkson.

Vellum bindings as surfaces for decoration have been utilized to great pictorial effect by Edwards of Halifax in the eighteenth century (fig. 72) and, more recently, in a non-traditional manner, by Trevor Jones (fig. 87). The work of Sydney M. Cockerell and Joan Rix Tebbutt in toned vellum ornamented with inked scribework and gold stamping is a notable contemporary treatment of this traditional material (fig. 13).

12. GOLD-STAMPED VELLUM BINDING   *ca. 1580*

Horae Beatae Mariae Virginis. Illuminated manuscript on vellum. Ca. 1500.

Limp vellum, gold-stamped. Made paper and vellum endpapers; edges gilt. Single cream and yellow linen endbands; flat back. 183 x 122 mm.

At one time this binding was thought to have been owned by Diane de Poitiers, on the basis of the interlaced cypher of 2 Ds and an H, but that attribution is debatable as the binding lacks the crescents, bows and other symbols of Diana and the crowned H commonly associated with her bindings. The concentric borders of H-D cypher also include a double lambda interlaced with an H which may refer to Henri III, the letters standing for Henri, Louise and Lorraine, as suggested by Olivier.

PROVENANCE: Leather bookplate of Robert Hoe, printed label of Templeton Crocker.

REFERENCES: Olivier et al., *Manuel,* pl. 2491. Ricci, *Census,* vol. I, p. 30. Cf. Miner, *History of bookbinding,* nos. 339 and 340 for similar concentric borders of cyphers.

Hunt Library, from the original collection of Rachel McMasters Miller Hunt

13. SYDNEY M. COCKERELL AND JOAN RIX TEBBUTT   *1976*

The four gospels of the Lord Jesus Christ, according to the authorized version of King James I with decoration by Eric Gill. London, Golden Cockerell Press, 1931.

Toned vellum, stamped in gold with black scribe work. Green endpapers and black morocco doublures; gilt edges. Single gold and light blue endbands, smooth spine. 335 x 235 mm. Signed: 19 SC [monogram] JT 76

Designed and executed by Sydney M. Cockerell, binder, and Joan Rix Tebbutt, scribe.

Sydney Morris Cockerell, born in 1906, is the son of the bookbinder Douglas Cockerell, with whom he went into partnership in 1924. He learned bookbinding from his father at an early age and also attended the Central School of Arts and Crafts, where later he taught for many years. He was also a teacher at the Royal College of Art, and has lectured and written extensively on bookbinding. His book, *The repairing of books,* was first published in 1958. Well known for his work in book conservation, he is also largely responsible for the recent revival and further development of the art of marbling paper.

Joan Rix Tebbutt is a scribe who teaches at the Glasgow School of Art and has worked with Cockerell for many years. The designs for their vellum bindings originate with her and then are developed through mutual discussion. She does all the black ink work on the bindings. The gold work is done by Cockerell, using a special pneumatic blocking press, which he designed and built from an aircraft ram, and a guided heated fillet for running the gold lines between the black ones.

REFERENCE: Harrop, "Craft binders at work IV."

Bridwell Library, Southern Methodist University

STRAPWORK AND ARABESQUES

Gold tooling was introduced from the Eastern world, probably through Venice in the mid-fifteenth century. It quickly became established in France and reached a peak in the sixteenth century with the binders who worked for the courts of France and the renowned bibliophiles Jean Grolier and Thomas Mahieu.

The designs of these gold-tooled bindings reflect the influence of the Eastern world. The knotted and interlacing strapwork motif and the floral arabesque work were found in Moslem art and architecture as well as on the covers of books. In Europe also, these designs were not confined to bookbinding. Pattern books of Eastern arabesque designs served various crafts in sixteenth century Europe, and these motifs appeared in the type designs of Geoffroy Tory and the parterres of Vignola. The interlacing strapwork in a fanfare design, in vogue as a binding design in the 1570s, made earlier appearances elsewhere, most notably in the illustration of the knight in fanfare armor in Jacques Roffet's 1549 publication of L'entrée de Henri II à Paris.

In the twentieth century, bookbinders have used the strapwork motif in the traditional manner to capture a sense of the past, as in the Gunner binding (fig. 20), or on the genealogical work by the American Historical Company (fig. 67). The design of a recent binding by Faith Shannon on a seventeenth century gardening book uses strapwork to represent a maze, popular in that century for garden plans as well as bindings.[1] These historic motifs are often translated into twentieth century aesthetics, as in the MacLeish binding with an art nouveau treatment (fig. 22), and in the de Sauty binding with a contemporary linear motif (fig. 17).

---

[1]*Designer bookbinders 3,* p. 35.

14. COMMISSIONED BY JEAN GROLIER   *16th century*

Arnobius Afer. *Arnobii disputationum adversus gentes libri octo.* Rome, apud F. Priscianen, 1542.

Plate no. 6 from: Antoine Jean Victor Le Roux de Lincy. *Recherches sur Jean Grolier sur sa vie et sa bibliothèque.* Paris, 1866.

Tan calf, black paint, gold-tooled. Grolier motto and inscription on lower cover: "Portio mea domine sit in terra viventium." and "Io. Grolierii et amicorum."

Antoine Jean Victor Le Roux de Lincy (1806-1869) was a nineteenth century Parisian bibliographer whose fame was established by his study of the life and library of Jean Grolier, including compilation of a list of Grolier volumes and an account of their ownership.

REFERENCE: Le Roux de Lincy, *Recherches sur Jean Grolier,* no. 18. Shipman, *Researches concerning Jean Grolier,* no. 30.

Hunt Library, from the original collection of Rachel McMasters Miller Hunt

15. CLUB BINDERY   *1906*

Robert Burton. *The anatomy of melancholy.* Oxford, printed by John Litchfield and James Short for Henry Cripps, 1621.

Blue crushed levant morocco, rust and olive morocco onlays, gold tooling. Marbled endpapers, blue morocco doublures; rough gilt edges. Single red and yellow silk endbands; five raised bands. 194 x 140 mm. Signed: The Club Bindery 1906, Leon Maillard, Finisher

Large paper copy with rare leaf of errata.

Resembles the interlaced knotwork designs of the mudjar bindings.

The Club Bindery was founded in 1895 by Edwin Holden, members of the Grolier Club, and other wealthy bibliophiles in order to bring to America the fine craft of hand bookbinding. Leon Maillard, who had worked for Cuzin, Gruel and Marius Michel, was one of the French craftsmen imported to work in the bindery.

While designs of the Club Bindery bindings tended to follow traditional styles, the craftsmanship was exquisite. Robert Hoe, its most influential manager and client, was concerned not with the art of binding design, but with the quality of the binding and the condition of the text: "After all that can be said in favor of retaining books in their original covers, there are very many which for their preservation demand rebinding . . . Every collector cannot do otherwise than consider himself . . . as temporary custodian." The Club Bindery closed in 1909.

PROVENANCE: Leather bookplates of Robert Hoe (sale 1911/12, pt. 3, no. 516) and Beverly Chew. Bookplate of C. J. Rosenbloom.

REFERENCE: Thompson and Thompson, *Fine binding in America*, p. 10.

Special Collections Department, University of Pittsburgh Libraries

16. RACHEL McMASTERS MILLER HUNT *1917-1918*

Washington Irving. *Old Christmas*. London, Macmillan, 1892.

Dark green crushed levant morocco, red leather onlays, gold tooling. Red, green and white Italian woodblock endpapers; gilt edges. Double red and green silk endbands; projecting endcaps, five raised bands. 255 x 178 mm. Signed: [lamb] RMcMM 1917

REFERENCE: Titcombe, *Bookbinding career*, no. 112.

Hunt Botanical Library

17. ALFRED DE SAUTY *1929*

Pierre de Ronsard. *Songs & sonnets of Pierre de Ronsard, gentleman of Vendomois,* selected & translated into English verse by Curtis Hidden Page, with an introductory essay & notes. Boston & New York, Houghton, Mifflin and Company, 1903.

Green levant morocco, red and black niger onlays, gold tooling. Maroon niger doublures with black niger border, gold tooling; made endpapers of maroon niger and hand-colored green, pink and black paper; top edge gilt. Single red and green silk endbands. Five raised bands. 192 x 110 mm. Signed: Donnelley—Chicago

Designed by Alfred de Sauty.

The Extra Bindery at the Lakeside Press, of the firm R. R. Donnelley & Sons, was established in 1921. Its ideals of quality of material and suitability of design were those put forward by Douglas Cockerell and others of the Arts and Crafts Movement. The department was staffed with finishers chosen by Douglas Cockerell, and late in 1923 came under the direction of Alfred de Sauty.

The designs, as seen in a catalogue of bindings published by Donnelley's in 1925, are conservative renditions of traditional patterns. By contrast, in 1929 Donnelley's published *A rod for the back of the binder,* in which the firm stated that "we have ventured into new fields of design . . . which we trust will lead to the evolution of a distinctly characteristic style of our own."

REFERENCE: *A rod for the back of the binder,* p. [32].

Binding and information on de Sauty, courtesy of the Graphic Conservation Department, R. R. Donnelley & Sons Company

18. CLAUDE DE PICQUES? *1540s*

Marinus Barletius. *De vita moribus ac rebus praecipue adversus Turcas gestis, Georgii Castrioti, clarrissimi Epirotarum principis, qui propter celeberrima facinora, Scanderbegus, hoc est, Alexander Magnus, cognominatus fuit* . . . Strasbourg, apud Cratonem Mylium, 1537.

Brown calf, gold-tooled. Plain endpapers; gilt edges. Single gold and green silk endbands (19th century); six raised bands, rebacked. 334 x 210 mm.

Grolier motto "Portio mea domine sit in terra viventium" on lower cover. Spine repaired and tooled to its condition of 1650 when the volume was part of the library of Dominique de Vic.

Probably bound by Claude de Picques, one of the French royal binders who also bound for Jean Grolier. Many of the bindings that de Picques executed for Grolier were worked in this interlacing lozenge and rectangle design. Jean Grolier, 1479-1565, the French statesman and bibliophile, by virtue of the extent of his library and his unmistakable marks of ownership, is remembered as the foremost book collector of all times. "Because of the infinite variety of designs which he originated and caused to be executed for him, and the richness of ornamentation which he demanded, he was a pioneer in the art of bookbinding." —Baron Roger Portalis.

PROVENANCE: Dominique de Vic, Seth Sprague Terry.

REFERENCES: Maggs, *Catalogue 407,* no. 86; *Catalogue 489,* no. 65. Shipman, *Researches concerning Jean Grolier,* no. 39, p. xvi. Austin, *The library of Jean Grolier,* no. 39. Nixon, *16th century gold-tooled bookbindings,* pp. 37-39.

Library of the Grolier Club of New York

19. DOVES BINDERY *1919*

Johann Wolfgang von Goethe. *Torquato Tasso, ein Schauspiel.* Hammersmith, Doves Press, 1913.

Blue morocco, gold-tooled. Plain endpapers; gilt edges. Double olive green silk endbands; five raised bands, projecting endcaps. 234 x 171 mm. Signed: The · Doves · Bindery 19 C-S 19

Executed by the firm of C. and C. MacLeish and identical to a 1913 Doves binding on *Torquato Tasso* pictured as no. 250 in Maggs, *Catalogue 966.*

After the closing of the Doves Bindery in 1909, Charles McLeisch went into partnership with his son. He had worked for Rivière before coming to work for Cobden-Sanderson, as a finisher. His son, Charles, had been apprenticed under Roger de Coverly. While the craftsmanship of

44

this binding is excellent, the design lacks the inspiration of those the MacLeisches produced under their own name.

PROVENANCE: Blue leather bookplate of C. C. Kalbfleisch.

REFERENCE: Nixon, *Broxbourne*, p. 230.

Hunt Library, from the original collection of Rachel McMasters Miller Hunt

20. JEAN GUNNER   *1964*

Walter James Turner, ed. *Impressions of English literature.* London, Collins, 1947.

Blue niger morocco, gold-tooled. Marbled endpapers; top edge gilt. Single light blue silk endbands; five raised bands. 226 x 168 mm.

Jean Gunner

21. GEOMETRIC COMPARTMENT PATTERN
16th century

Valerius Maximus nuper editus: Index copiosissimus rerum omnium et personarum de quibus in his libris agitur. Venice, in aed. haered. Aldi et Andreae soceri, 1534.

Plate no. 5 from: Antoine Jean Victor Le Roux de Lincy. *Recherches sur Jean Grolier sur sa vie et sa bibliothèque.* Paris, 1866.

While retaining the basic strapwork and arabesque elements of what has become known as the Grolier style, geometric compartment patterns, such as on the binding exhibited here, illustrate the origin of the primitive fanfare motif; this motif later developed into the repetitious compartmentalized treatment of the full fanfare design.

REFERENCES: Le Roux de Lincy, *Recherches sur Jean Grolier,* no. 317. Shipman, *Researches concerning Jean Grolier,* no. 515.

Hunt Library, from the original collection of Rachel McMasters Miller Hunt

22. CHARLES McLEISCH   *1909*

Dante Gabriel Rossetti. *Hand and soul.* Hammersmith, Kelmscott Press, 1895.

Red morocco, olive green onlays, gold tooling. Plain endpapers; gilt edges. Single olive green endbands; five raised bands. 143 x 104 mm. Signed: C · McL-1909

Interlaced strapwork in early fanfare design. A flowing floral pattern gives an art nouveau flavor to the sixteenth century fanfare outline.

Hunt Library, from the original collection of Rachel McMasters Miller Hunt

23. RACHEL McMASTERS MILLER HUNT   *1911*

The life of Benvenuto Cellini, written by himself. New York, Brentano's, 1906.

Dark blue seal, red onlays, gold tooling. "Old Italian" gold on black endpapers and doublures; gilt and gauffered edges. Double green silk endbands; projecting endcaps, five raised bands. 227 x 167 mm. Signed: RMcMM · 1911

Italianate tools were used here to produce a primitive fan-

fare design after those executed for Mahieu, De Thou and others by several Paris ateliers in the mid-1560s. The arms above and below the central compartment resemble those of the Medici. The salamander and crown at the sides represent the arms of François I. Mrs. Hunt captured the spirit of Cellini's age, yet avoided producing an imitation of the Paris ateliers.

References: Titcombe, *Bookbinding career,* no. 51. Nixon, *16th century gold-tooled bookbindings,* pp. 172-175.

Hunt Botanical Library

SEMIS BINDINGS

The semis design, an all-over repeating figure pattern, is believed to have been taken from textiles. A medieval reference to its use is quoted by A. R. A. Hobson from the duc de Berry's inventories of 1404-1407.[1] In binding design its use was popularized by the sixteenth century binding shop of Nicholas and Clovis Eve and their work for the reigning kings of France. Nicholas Eve is known to have been responsible for the bindings on forty-two copies of the Statutes of the Order of the Saint-Espirit which were gold-tooled to a semis pattern of alternate flames and fleurs-de-lis.[2] The semis became a standard design pattern and, although its use in binding design fell off for a period after the first part of the seventeenth century, it surfaced again and again utilizing the popular figures of the day. In the twentieth century, with an emphasis on the representational aspects of design, the figure is more frequently chosen for its relation to the text.

[1]Hobson, A.R.A., *French and Italian collectors,* p. 65.
[2]Nixon, *16th century gold-tooled bookbindings,* no. 57.

24. CLOVIS EVE?   *late 16th to early 17th century*

Jeronymo Osorio. *Silvensis episcopi, de gloria libri V. Eiusdem de nobilitate civili & Christiana, libri V.* Cologne, apud Gosuinum Cholinum, 1595.

Brown calf, green and black paint, gold tooling. Plain endpapers; gilt and gauffered edges. Single yellow, gold and green silk endbands; smooth spine, rebacked with original spine replaced. Evidence of two pairs of ties. 135 x 78 mm.

A semis of fleurs-de-lis forms a background for the central cartouche of laurel branches.

Nicolas and Clovis Eve, believed to be father and son, were royal binders to Kings Henri III, Henri IV and Louis XIII, probably spanning the period from 1572 to 1634.

PROVENANCE: Bookplate of Henry William Poor.

REFERENCE: Nixon, *16th century gold-tooled bookbindings,* p. 220.

Hunt Library, from the original collection of Rachel McMasters Miller Hunt

25. THOMAS J. COBDEN-SANDERSON   *1885*

[Pseudo-Bonaventura.] *Meditatione sopra la passione.* Venice, Matteo Capcasa, 1490.

Red levant morocco, gold-tooled. Plain endpapers; rough

gilt edges. Turn-ins gold-tooled with trellis border design. Single red silk endbands. Smooth spine. 208 x 162 mm. Signed: 1885 Cobden-Sanderson.

Executed for Charles Fairfax Murray, who was displeased that the back had been cut and guarded like a manuscript. Bain, the bookseller, however, appreciated the fine craftsmanship, found the binding "staid and appropriate," and felt that Cobden-Sanderson's "name would be in the future, a hundred years hence."

PROVENANCE: C. Fairfax Murray; bookplates of C. W. Dyson Perrins, and of Sir Robert Leighton.

REFERENCES: Adams, *T. J. Cobden-Sanderson*, no. 9, pl. 4. Cobden-Sanderson, *Journals*, vol. 1, pp. 232, 393.

Hunt Library, from the original collection of Rachel McMasters Miller Hunt

26. SANGORSKI AND SUTCLIFFE   *ca. 1906-1923*

Robert Browning. *Rabbi Ben Ezra.* London, Grolier Society, n.d.

Citron morocco, blue morocco onlays, white and green onlays, gold tooling, four opals. Cream moiré silk endpapers, cream morocco doublures with inlays of green rose leaves; rough gilt edges. Red and green silk endbands; five raised bands. 250 x 180 mm. Signed: Bound by Sangorski & Sutcliffe, London

Illuminated manuscript on vellum, possibly by Alberto Sangorski. Colophon: This copy of Rabbi Ben Ezra by Robert Browning was especially written out, illuminated, and bound by hand, and will not be duplicated. The Grolier Society, London.

Francis Sangorski and George Sutcliffe, students of Douglas Cockerell, founded their own atelier in 1901. Their lavish use of colored leathers, gold, and semi-precious stones, combined with oriental motifs, resulted in bindings of great richness of detail. This semis of peacock eyes is a variation on their jewelled peacock bindings, the first completed in 1903 and exhibited in 1905 in Frankfurt-am-Main. The peacock design was frequently used on copies of the *Rubáiyát of Omar Khayyám.*

PROVENANCE: Phoebe Boyle (sale, 19-20 November 1923, no. 55).

REFERENCE: Elkind, "Jewelled bindings."

From the Collection of Charles J. Rosenbloom

27. THOMAS W. PATTERSON   *1959*

Botanical books, prints & drawings from the collection of Mrs. Roy Arthur Hunt. Pittsburgh, Department of Fine Arts, Carnegie Institute, 1952.

Turquoise blue oasis, gold-tooled. Blue marbled endpapers and blue marbled doublures bordered with gold-tooled navy inlays; top edge gilt. Double black and white silk endbands; five raised bands. 232 x 155 mm. Signed: Thos. W. Patterson—1959.

REFERENCE: *Thomas W. Patterson, bookbinder,* no. 34.

Hunt Botanical Library, from the original collection of Rachel McMasters Miller Hunt

28. WILLIAM MATTHEWS   *1970*

Antonio de Guevera. *The praise and happinesse of the countrie-life.* Newtown, Gregynog Press, 1938.

Brown oasis, gold-tooled. Cloudy gray stained endpapers; gilt edges. Single red silk endbands; two raised bands. 183 x 120 mm. Signed: 19 WFM 70.

John M. Wing Foundation, The Newberry Library

29. MICHAEL WILCOX   *1979*

Robert Norman. *The newe attractive, shewing the nature, propertie, and manifold vertues of the loadstone; with the declination of the needle, touched therewith, under the plaine of the horizon.* London, 1720.

Maroon oasis, gold-tooled. Plain endleaves; original stained edges. Single rose-beige and white linen endbands; five raised bands. 192 x 124 mm. Signed: Wilcox

Michael Wilcox, born in 1939, was apprenticed to several bookbinders in Bristol for five years and to George Bayntun of Bath for one year. After moving to Canada in 1962, he worked as a preparator in mammalogy at the Natural History Department of the Royal Ontario Museum. He established his bookbinding studio in 1969 and is currently involved in the restoration of a collection of early medical books for the University of Toronto.

A semis effect is achieved here using star and moon tools cut by the binder especially for this design. Celestial tools and dotted backgrounds were common in English Restoration bindings and Scottish bindings of the same period. In the next century the Irish used various small tools, including stars and moons, to achieve this same semis effect.

Canadian Coast Guard College Library

REPETITION MOSAIC

The repetition mosaic designs are an extension of the French tradition of binding design of the sixteenth and seventeenth centuries—the semis and the strapwork patterns which developed into the fanfare motifs. The design is an all-over repeating one of geometric patterns, of colored onlays surrounded and connected by meandering fillets.

The repetition mosaic motif is often used by modern French binders, but the period effect is avoided because the geometric patterns are non-figurative and can be very representative of twentieth century aesthetics.

30. ANTOINE-MICHEL PADELOUP   *ca. 1730-1740*

Giovanni Boccaccio. *Il Decamerone.* Florence, Philippo de Giunta, 1527.

Citron morocco, olive and red morocco onlays, gold tooling. Gilt endpapers, red morocco doublures, gold-tooled; gilt edges. Red, yellow, green and brown silk endbands; five raised bands. 193 x 135 mm.

Worked in a repetition mosaic design.

Antoine-Michel Padeloup, called Padeloup le jeune, is reputed to be the originator of the repetition mosaic designs on leather bindings. His use of the design is another clear example of the integral relationships of the art of binding and the popular motifs of the day. Louis-Marie Michon stated in his work on mosaic bindings of the eighteenth century: "[Padeloup] transposait ainsi sur le cuir certains décors de pavements ou de boiseries du début de siècle," and one must add to that the marquetry patterns in French furniture of the day. While the Padeloup atelier is the one generally associated with repetition mosaic bindings, other ateliers of the eighteenth century, most notably that of the family Derome, used the design.

PROVENANCE: Camus de Limare (sale 1786), 6th Duke of Buccleuch (sale 1889), James Toovey, Pierpont Morgan (1899).

REFERENCES: Morgan, *Toovey catalogue*, illus. facing p. 88. Michon, *Les reliures mosaïquées*, pp. 29, 64 (no. 28). Harthan, *Bookbindings*, p. 18.

The Pierpont Morgan Library, New York

31. RACHEL McMASTERS MILLER HUNT — *1918*

Thomas Gray. *Poems*. Parma, Bodoni, 1793.

Turquoise blue crushed levant morocco, gold- and blind-tooled. Blue wood-blocked endpapers; rough gilt edges. Double olive green silk endbands; projecting endcaps, five raised bands. 257 x 180 mm. Signed: [lamb] RMcMM · 1918

The dark blind tooling of the coved diamond-shaped interstices is used to obtain the onlaid effect characteristic of repetition mosaic bindings. While the overall effect is very modern, the design bears surprisingly close resemblance to a repetition mosaic binding on *Almanach royal*, 1746, pictured on Plate XLIII in Michon's *Les reliures mosaïquées*.

REFERENCE: Titcombe, *Bookbinding career*, no. 113.

Hunt Botanical Library

32. HENRI CREUZEVAULT — *20th century*

Charles Pierre Baudelaire. *Vingt-sept poèmes des fleurs du mal, illustrés par Rodin*. Paris, Imprimé pour la Société des "Amis du livre moderne," 1918.

Yellow morocco, onlays of red, black, blue and green morocco, white paint, gold and blind tooling. Black suede endleaves, brown morocco doublures; gilt edges. Double yellow and brown silk endbands; smooth spine. 184 x 118 mm. Signed: Creuzevault

Errata slip gives correct title: Vingt-cinq poèmes de Baudelaire, illustrés de vingt-sept dessins de Rodin.

Henri Creuzevault (1905-1971) learned the art of fine bookbinding, forwarding and finishing in his father's atelier and did not confine himself to the design aspect of binding until later in his life. Creuzevault, also a publisher of finely illustrated books, eventually left the field altogether to become the director of an art gallery. The design of the binding exhibited here, an asymmetrical use of repetition mosaic, illustrates the union of modern art and historic tradition. For a modern symmetrical use of this pattern by Pierre Legrain, see the sale catalogue *Livres illustrés & oeuvres originales* of Drouot Rive Gauche, Paris, 1978.

REFERENCES: Miner, *History of bookbinding*, pp. 253-254.

Drouot Rive Gauche, *Livres illustrés & oeuvres originales*, no. 39.

John M. Wing Foundation, The Newberry Library

RESTORATION BINDINGS

The restoration of the monarchy in England initiated an era of brilliantly gold-tooled leather bindings that were distinctly English. Theretofore the Parisian ateliers had dominated in skill and power of design. In the second half of the seventeenth century, new finishing tools were cut in England which were used to create new design motifs like the cottage roof and the all-over drawer handle, as well as to revitalize the standard rectangular patterns. Joyous release from puritanical rule was expressed in the heavy gold tooling, the leaf sprays and floral tools against backgrounds made vivid through the use of paint and colored leathers.

DRAWER-HANDLE STYLE

The drawer-handle tool takes its shape from the Greek Ionic columns and the form appears in a less defined manner in some of the earlier pointilliste tooling of the sixteenth century. Under the Dutch influence in Restoration England, single heavy finishing tools were cut into this form and the drawer handle figure became the main element in an all-over floral design. This figured tool continued to appear in various forms throughout the eighteenth and nineteenth centuries, but never as the dominant feature after the Restoration period.

33. THE QUEEN'S BINDER? — *ca. 1673*

Richard Allestree. *The ladies calling*. Oxford, printed at the Theatre, 1673.

Black turkey, gold-tooled. Marbled endpapers; gilt edges. Double red, white and blue silk endbands; five raised bands. 185 x 119 mm.

This binding was probably executed by one of the Queen's Binders, since their drawer-handle designs included such pointilliste volutes, and the distinctive floral tool of four petals and two leaves.

PROVENANCE: Inscription of M. T. Bond, 1764. Bookplate of William and Leonora Sophia Buller.

REFERENCES: Nixon, *English Restoration bookbindings*, pp. 32-37. Hobson, G. D., *Bindings in Cambridge libraries*, pp. 144-145, pl. LVIII.

Hunt Library, from the original collection of Rachel McMasters Miller Hunt

34. JEAN GUNNER — *1979*

Nehemiah Grew. *The anatomy of vegetables begun*. London, printed for S. Hickman, 1672.

Black oasis, gold-tooled. Plain endpapers; original red and black sprinkled edges. Single pink and white silk endbands; five bands. 162 x 98 mm. Signed: J. Gunner 1979

The modern drawer handle tool was cut by the binder especially for this binding.

Hunt Botanical Library

The cottage-roof style was derived by applying elements of Dutch gabled architecture to the coved panel design popular in France earlier in the century. Elaborate naturalistic foliage and floral tools used in the design were the distinctive marks of the English Restoration binders.

35. COTTAGE-ROOF BINDING   *17th century*

Thomas Flatman. *Poems and songs.* London, printed by S. and B. G. for Benjamin Took . . . and Jonathan Edwin, 1674.

Red turkey, gold-tooled. Marbled endpapers; gilt edges. Single blue, pink and white silk endbands; five raised bands. Rebacked with original spine replaced. 176 x 112 mm.

A cottage-roof design using pointilliste, solid and azured tooling. Many of the tools are similar to those of the Mearne shop, but the quality of the tooling is uneven and in some places the tooling has cut into the leather.

Samuel Mearne (1624-1683) became Bookbinder to the King upon the restoration of the monarchy in 1660. Prior to that he spent some time in Holland and, later, his London shop included at least one Dutchman, Suckerman, an excellent craftsman who is thought to have been the foreman. Mearne, also involved in bookselling and publishing and an active member of the Stationers' Company, probably did not devote much time to actual bookbinding. However, his two sons, Charles and Samuel, were also binders and the younger, Charles, was in partnership with his father and succeeded to the shop upon his death.

PROVENANCE: Armorial bookplate of Lord Viscount Powerscourt. Tiffany bookplate of William Hartman Woodin, with American Numismatic Society printed at the top.

REFERENCES: Nixon, *English Restoration bookbindings,* pp. 10-12; *Broxbourne,* pp. 150-151. Maggs, *Catalogue 966,* p. 57.

Hunt Library, from the original collection of Rachel McMasters Miller Hunt

36. JEAN GUNNER   *1978*

Caspar Commelin. *Praeludia botanica ad publicas plantarum exoticarum demonstrationes.* Leyden, F. Haringh, 1703.

Red oasis, black oasis onlays, gold tooling. Plain endpapers; original gilt edges. Single red and white silk endbands; five raised bands. 267 x 212 mm. Signed: J. Gunner 1978

This use of red and black leather with gold-tooled floral designs conveys the spirit of English Restoration bindings.

PROVENANCE: Bookplate of the Earl of Aylesford dating from about 1779.

REFERENCE: *Hunt catalogue,* no. 405.

Hunt Botanical Library, from the original collection of Rachel McMasters Miller Hunt

37. IVOR ROBINSON   *1976*

Final design for binding on: *The life and times of Anthony à Wood—Antiquary of Oxford—1632-1695.* Oxford, Oxford Polytechnic, 1975.

Dark blue oasis, gold-tooled. Dark blue oasis doublures, pale yellow suede flyleaves and marbled endpapers; rough gilt edges. Five raised bands. 225 x 145 mm.

Number 1 of 100 copies printed at the Department of Design, Oxford Polytechnic.

Tooled to a linear cottage design for presentation to Queen Elizabeth II at the opening of the new Oxfordshire County Hall in Oxford, March, 1976. "Anthony Wood was an Oxford don of the 17th century who was almost an exact contemporary of the great Oxford cottage binder, Roger Bartlett." . . . I. Robinson.

Ivor Robinson worked his first cottage binding in 1953 on *Came to Oxford* by Gertrude and Muirhead Bone. His cottage bindings capture in modern linear terms the heaviness of Restoration design and contrast with the movement and spatial freedom of his non-traditionally based designs.

Ivor Robinson, with permission of Her Majesty, Queen Elizabeth II

38. RESTORATION PANEL BINDING   *ca. 1717*

The Holy Bible, containing the Old Testament and the New: Newly translated out of the original tongues: and with the former translations diligently compared and revised by His Majesty's Special Command. Oxford, printed by John Baskett, Printer to the King's most Excellent Majesty, for Great Britain; and to the University, 1717. Volume one of two.

Dark blue morocco, gold-tooled. Marbled endpapers; rough gilt edges. Double multicolored endbands; eight raised bands. Two pairs of ties added at the fore-edge. 506 x 372 mm.

This edition is known as the Vinegar Bible because of a typographical error in the spelling of vineyard in the heading of Luke, chapter 20.

While the general design of the binding is in the Restoration panel style, the tools used, most notably the rolls, are from the early eighteenth century when that style was still popular.

PROVENANCE: Purchased from the estate of the Earl of Onslow by Arthur F. Grafflin and given to the Pittsburgh Theological Seminary in memory of his mother, Margaret Cassell Grafflin.

Pittsburgh Theological Seminary

39. WILLIAM MATTHEWS   *1969*

The Holy Bible. Containing the Old and New Testaments and the books called Apocrypha. London, Oxford University Press [1960/61?].

Dark blue-green morocco, gold-tooled. Vellum doublures and endpapers; gilt edges. Double beige linen endbands; five raised bands. 305 x 230 mm. Signed: W. Matthews 1969

Colophon: Printed in Great Britain at The University Press, Oxford, by Vivian Ridler.

The corner tooling is reminiscent of eighteenth century dentelle work, although the overall effect is of the Restoration period. The modern arabesque tools and rolls place the design in the twentieth century.

From the collection of Mr. and Mrs. Douglas G. Moore

RECTANGULAR BINDINGS

Given the prevailing shape of the book, all binding designs can be said to be rectangular. The styles known specifically as rectangular are those which emphasize the shape of the covers, calling attention to it by simple outline in fillets, by defining that outline in borders of tooling or contrasting panels, or by highlighting the edges with a center and corner design. Though often unobtrusive and even severe, the designs based on these distribution schemes can also be elaborate, as with the border binding by Pierre-Lucien Martin (fig. 49).

BORDERS AND PANELS

As early as the fifteenth century, bindings were decorated with concentric rectangular borders blind-tooled using individual tools or rolls. For a sixteenth century example of this style with a central panel stamp, see fig. 5. In later periods the same border effect was achieved with gilt fillets. Painting or sprinkling the leather in alternate borders produced a panelled effect popular in the eighteenth century. Arabesques and fleurons often were used to accent the corners. Typical of seventeenth and eighteenth century border treatment were the bindings à la dentelle executed with great skill by such binders as the Derome family and Roger Payne.

40. ROGER PAYNE   *ca. 1764*

Horace Walpole. *A catalogue of the royal and noble authors of England, with a list of their works.* London, printed for R. and J. Dodsley, and J. Graham, 1759. Volume one of two.

Red straight-grained morocco, gold-tooled. Marbled endpapers; gilt edges. Double green, beige and brown silk endbands; five raised bands. 190 x 120 mm.

Evidence gathered by Howard Nixon indicates that this binding is an early example of Roger Payne's work, probably done while he was still at Eton. Several of the tools used here are those found on the doublures of an early signed Payne binding from the Sir Geoffrey Keynes Collection. The rather stiff dentelle is typical of the period rather than characteristic of the later, more distinctive style of the binder.

Roger Payne (1738-1797) was the most influential English binder of the eighteenth century. He studied binding in Eton, went to London in 1766, where he was greatly assisted by his patron, Thomas Payne, for the rest of his life. Much known for his elaborate gold tooling, especially in the decoration of the spines, he also earned some renown for his equally elaborate and detailed bills and tickets.

PROVENANCE: Collection of Mr. and Mrs. Valerian Lada-Mocarski.

REFERENCES: Nixon, *Broxbourne,* no. 96; "English bookbindings XLV;" *Five centuries,* no. 72.

Arts of the Book Collection, Yale University

41. NICOLAS DEROME   *ca. 1760*

Novum Jesu Christi testamentum, vulgatae editionis. Paris, e Typographia Regia, 1649. Volume one of two.

Red morocco, gold-tooled. Marbled endpapers; gilt edges. Double white, blue and pink silk endbands; five raised

bands. 144 x 80 mm. Binder's ticket: Relie par DeRome, rue des Chiens, près Ste. Geneviéve, a Paris.

An example of the *dentelles à l'oiseau,* using the characteristic small bird tool, by the second son of Jacques Antoine Derome, and brother to the celebrated Nicolas Denis Derome, called le jeune.

Royal Library, The Hague, The Netherlands

42. JEAN GUNNER   *1979*

Albrecht von Haller. *Icones plantarum helvetiae.* Bern, sumptibus Societatis Typographicae, 1795.

Tan oasis morocco, gold-tooled. Tan, beige and blue-gray marbled endpapers. Double blue and pink silk endbands; six raised bands. 427 x 282 mm. Signed: J. Gunner 1979

Hunt Botanical Library

43. JEAN GUNNER   *1979*

Samuel Gottlieb Gmelin. *Historia fucorum.* Leningrad, ex typographia academiae scientiorum, 1768.

Maroon oasis, gold and black tooling. Maroon, gray and green marbled endpapers; original plain edges. Single maroon and green silk endbands; smooth spine. 282 x 225 mm. Signed: J. Gunner 1979

A tailored twentieth century rendering of a traditional lacework pattern.

Hunt Botanical Library

44. DOVES BINDERY   *1908*

Ralph Waldo Emerson. *Essays.* Hammersmith, Doves Press, 1906.

Dark blue morocco, gold-tooled. Plain endpapers. Double olive silk endbands; projecting endcaps, five raised bands. 235 x 165 mm. Signed: The · Doves · Bindery 19 C-S 08

PROVENANCE: Inscribed on back fly-leaf "Bound for Rachel McMasters Miller C S 28 Sep. 1908."

Hunt Library, from the original collection of Rachel McMasters Miller Hunt

45. RACHEL McMASTERS MILLER HUNT   *1910*

Edmund Spenser. *Epithalamion.* London, Essex House Press, 1901.

Rose crushed levant morocco, white and green onlays, gold tooling. Rose marbled endpapers; gilt edges. Double pink and green silk endbands; projecting endcaps, four raised bands. Gold clasp. 186 x 140 mm. Signed: R McM M [lamb] 1910

REFERENCE: Titcombe, *Bookbinding career,* no. 44.

Hunt Library

46. JOHN F. GRABAU   *1930*

J. C. [17th century Dutch agricultural writer]. *De verstandige huys-houder.* Amsterdam, Cornelis Janszoon, 1661.

Brown niger, blind-tooled. Plain endpapers, red stained

edges. Double yellow and brown silk endbands; five raised bands. 202 x 157 mm. Signed: Grabau

John F. Grabau (1878-1948) came as assistant foreman to Elbert Hubbard's Roycroft Shop after an apprenticeship to a printing and bookbinding shop in Buffalo. He established his own studio for fine bookbinding in 1905, in which he worked until late in 1947. Grabau did a number of bindings for noted political and literary figures, as well as elaborate bindings for his own collection. His studio continued after his death under his wife's direction.

REFERENCES: Buffalo Fine Arts Academy, *Catalog*, no. 66. *Hunt catalogue*, no. 288.

Hunt Botanical Library, from the original collection of Rachel McMasters Miller Hunt

47. BERNARD C. MIDDLETON   *1978*

Sebastian Munster. *Dictionarium hebraicum*. Basel, apud Hier. Frobenium & Nic. Episcopium, 1548.

Dark red-brown native-dyed niger, blind-tooled. Plain endpapers. Single blue and white linen endbands; five raised bands. Brass clasps hinged on vellum covered with leather. 173 x 120 mm. Signed: M[monogram] [197]8

Bernard Middleton, born in 1924, writes extensively on the craft of bookbinding and book repair, both as a practitioner and a historian. The son of a forwarder employed at W. T. Morrell and at Sangorski and Sutcliffe, he studied at the Central School of Arts and Crafts and was later apprenticed to the bindery of His Majesty's Stationery Office at the British Museum. He established his own shop in 1953 after several years at the Royal College of Art with Roger Powell and at Zaehnsdorf, Ltd., His concern for bookbinding structures and material is apparent in his many publications, especially the recently reissued *A history of English craft bookbinding technique* and the American Library Association's handbook *The restoration of leather bindings*.

REFERENCE: Harrop, "Craft binders at work VIII."

Bernard C. Middleton

48. THOMAS W. PATTERSON   *1957-1958*

Irish Room. *Donor's book*, Crafton, 1957-1958.

Dark green oasis morocco, light green inlays, gold tooling. Mossy green endpapers, natural and light green oasis doublures with gold tooling; top edge gilt. Double green and gold silk endbands; six raised bands. 348 x 265 mm. Signed: Thomas W. Patterson

A manuscript calligraphed and illuminated by the binder. The colophon reads, ". . . written out, embellished and bound by Thomas W. Patterson in Crafton, Pa., 1957-8."

REFERENCES: Guild of Book Workers, *Exhibition*, pl. xviii. *Thomas W. Patterson, bookbinder*, no. 31.

Nationality Rooms, University of Pittsburgh

49. PIERRE-LUCIEN MARTIN   *1962*

Louis Aragon. *Les poètes, poème*. Paris, Gallimard, 1960.

Dark green morocco, polished calf onlays in shades of green, rose, pink, yellow, brown and blue, blind tooling.

Dark green suede endpapers and doublures; rough gilt edges. Double dark green silk endbands; smooth spine. 238 x 184 mm. Signed: P. L. Martin   Dated: 1962

Number 28 of 30 copies on vélin de Hollande.

A vigorous re-statement of the traditional rectangular panel style. A similar binding using differently colored onlays is described in *La reliure originale française*.

Pierre-Lucien Martin, born in 1913, studied at École Estienne and worked in several studios before opening his own in 1940. His designs are readily recognizable for their expert use of geometric shapes, colors and lines.

PROVENANCE: Bookplate of J. R. Abbey (Sotheby Sale, 2 June 1970, no. 2539); bought for the Royal Library by the Foundation of Friends of the Library.

REFERENCES: *Verslag omtrent de Koninklijke Bibliotheek*, p. 24. *Modern British and French bookbindings from the collection of J. R. Abbey*, no. 114. *La reliure originale française*, no. 83.

Royal Library, The Hague, The Netherlands

50. SPRINKLED PANEL BINDING   *ca. 18th century*

Hieronymus Brunschwig. *A most excellent and perfecte homish apothecarye or homely physick booke*. Cologne, Arnold Birckman, 1561.

Brown calf, sprinkled center panel, blind-tooled. Plain endpapers; red sprinkled edges. Single red and white linen endbands; five raised bands, rebacked. 297 x 197 mm.

While older examples of this panel style are sometimes staid, a brilliant modern adaptation was designed by Paul Bonet on Paul Valéry's *Poésies*, illustrated in a recent sale catalogue of Drouot Rive Gauche.

REFERENCES: *Hunt catalogue*, no. 84. Drouot Rive Gauche, *Livres illustrés & oeuvres originales*, no. 48.

Hunt Botanical Library, from the original collection of Rachel McMasters Miller Hunt

51. RIVIÈRE & SON   *20th century*

Nicolas de Bonnefons. *The French gardiner*. London, printed by J. M. for John Crooke, 1669.

Brown sprinkled calf, tan calf onlays, gold tooling. Plain endpapers; gilt edges. Single green, pink and purple silk endbands; five raised bands. 150 x 95 mm. Signed: Bound by Riviere & Son

Rivière & Son was founded in Bath in 1829 by Robert Rivière (1809-1882), a man of Hugenot descent whose father was a well-known drawing-master. The business was moved to London in 1840 where the high quality of workmanship quickly became established. Rivière excelled in the retrospective binding popular in the nineteenth century. One notable achievement was the binding of a series of 117 "imitations of historic bindings" for Lord Howard de Walden. Much work was also done in full leather, undecorated but for the spine and gold fillets on the covers. The most skilled craftsmen, however, were engaged on the higher quality work and many went on to become known in their own rights. The firm of Rivière & Son closed its doors in 1939 and the tools passed to Bayntun's of Bath.

REFERENCES: *Hunt catalogue*, no. 312. Prideaux, *Modern bookbindings*, pp. 13-14. Nixon, "English bookbindings LXXIX;" *Five centuries*, no. 98.

Hunt Botanical Library, from the original collection of Rachel McMasters Miller Hunt

52. RACHEL McMASTERS MILLER HUNT   *1909*

Bliss Carman. *Sappho*. Boston, L. C. Page, 1903.

Green levant morocco, gold-tooled. Green and lavender marbled endpapers; gilt edges. Double green silk endbands; projecting endcaps, five raised bands. 235 x 158 mm. Signed: R Mc M M [lamb] 1909

REFERENCE: Titcombe, *Bookbinding career*, no. 33.

Hunt Botanical Library

CENTER AND CORNER STYLES

The center and corner design is the basis for many styles. Various elements of these patterns, particularly the center medallions, were often prepared as single stamps, so that the effect of a complex pattern built up from individual tools could be achieved repeatedly with a minimum of effort. These gold-stamped panel bindings were popular London trade bindings in the second half of the sixteenth century. Elaborately built-up corner ornaments are an important part of many center and corner styles, including the seventeenth century fan and wheel designs.

53. STAMPED CENTER MEDALLION BINDING   *ca. 1555*

Leonhardt Fuchs. *De historia stirpium commentarii insignes*. Lyons, J. de Tournes and G. Gazeau, 1555.

Vellum, gold-blocked and -tooled. Plain endpapers, gilt and gauffered edges. Single pink and white linen endbands; five raised bands. Remains of two pairs of green ties. 128 x 80 mm.

The strapwork of the center medallion was block-stamped, rather than built up with individual tools.

PROVENANCE: Bookplate of Nordkirchen.

REFERENCE: *Hunt catalogue*, no. 74.

Hunt Botanical Library, from the original collection of Rachel McMasters Miller Hunt

54. DOUGLAS COCKERELL   *1900*

Frédéric Mistral. *Mireille; poème provençal*. Paris, Librairie Hachette et Cie, 1884.

Tan niger morocco, green, white and dark blue morocco onlays, gold tooling. Blue-gray endpapers; gilt edges. Single green silk endbands; five raised bands. 343 x 270 mm. Signed: 19 DC [monogram] 00

As an apprentice in the Doves Bindery from 1893 to 1898, Douglas Cockerell (1870-1945) acquired much practical knowledge of the structure and durability of bindings while repairing and rebinding William Morris' collection of early printed books. Cockerell was largely responsible for the tooling on the pigskin-bound Kelmscott Chaucers, working from Cobden-Sanderson's designs based on Morris' sketches. In 1897 he began teaching at the Central School

of Arts and Crafts. His *Bookbinding and the care of books*, first published in 1901, is still a standard textbook. He started his own bindery in 1898 and set up a workshop in Letchworth, Cambridge with his son, Sydney Morris Cockerell, in 1924. While Cockerell's designs show the Cobden-Sanderson influence, his use of linear patterns makes his bindings clearly distinguishable.

PROVENANCE: Purchased from American Art Association, 1938.

Buffalo and Erie County Public Library, Rare Book Room

55. JEAN GUNNER   *1978*

Crispijn van de Passe. *Hortus floridus*. Utrecht, Arnhem, 1614-1616.

Brown oasis, dark brown oasis inlays, gold tooling. Plain endpapers. Single red and gold silk endbands; smooth spine. 242 x 172 mm. Signed: J. Gunner 1978

The design recalls the gold-stamped London and Lyons bindings of the early seventeenth century.

REFERENCE: *Hunt catalogue*, no. 199.

Hunt Botanical Library, from the original collection of Rachel McMasters Miller Hunt

56. TOOLED FAN BINDING   *ca. 1600-1650*

Novum testamentum. Paris, Robert Estienne, 1569.

Brown morocco, gold-tooled. Plain endpapers; gilt edges. Double pink and blue silk endbands; smooth spine, traces of two pairs of green ties. 125 x 75 mm.

There is evidence of a lettering piece added over the fan design on the spine. The fan designs on this binding appear not to have been block-stamped but to have been built up from individual tools.

PROVENANCE: Signature of L. Godolphin. Bookplate of Milton, Peterborough, a house now owned by Earl Fitzwilliam. Given to the University of Rochester by Robert F. Metzdorf.

REFERENCES: Hobson, G. D., *English bindings*, no. 23. Cf. block stamps in Nixon, *Broxbourne*, nos. 59, 70.

Department of Rare Books, Manuscripts and Archives, University of Rochester Library

57. RAMAGE   *early 20th century*

Alfred Lord Tennyson. *Idylls of the king*. London, Macmillan, 1904.

Blue morocco, gold-tooled. Beige moiré silk endpapers and doublures; gilt edges. Single white silk endbands; five false raised bands. 161 x 108 mm. Signed: Bound by Ramage London

A twentieth century adaptation of the Scottish wheel design, which was an early eighteenth century variation of English and European fan designs of the previous century. The most notable difference between the Scottish wheel and the fan designs is the substitution of the stiff leaf sprays for the quarter fans at the corners. While the tool designs themselves are not those typically found on Scottish bindings, the general style is the same, comprising a center wheel, corner leaf sprays and pyramids of fish scales.

REFERENCES: Sommerlad, *Scottish 'wheel.'* Nixon, *Broxbourne,* no. 91.

Hunt Library, from the original collection of Rachel McMasters Miller Hunt

58. JEAN GUNNER   *1978*

John Parkinson. *Theatrum botanicum.* London, Thomas Cotes, 1640.

Medium green chieftan, gold-tooled. Plain endpapers. Double red and green silk endbands; six raised bands. 359 x 242 mm. Signed: J. Gunner 1978

This particular design is reminiscent of the English fan pattern, but was built up using 649 individual impressions rather than block-stamped as was more typical of seventeenth century fan bindings.

PROVENANCE: Armorial bookplate of the House of Commons Library; the original binding had the House's arms stamped on both covers.

REFERENCE: *Hunt catalogue,* no. 235.

Hunt Botanical Library, from the original collection of Rachel McMasters Miller Hunt

59. PAUL BONET   *1946*

Paul Valéry [*et al.*]. *Paul Bonet.* Paris, Librairie Auguste Blaizot, 1945.

Wine cape goat, gold-tooled. Rose beige box calf endpapers and doublures; rough gilt edges. Double red silk endbands; smooth spine. 335 x 252 mm. Signed: Paul Bonet   Dated: 1946

One of the irradiant bindings designed by Paul Bonet in which the traditional static wheel design is translated into a dynamic whorl.

PROVENANCE: From the collection of Laura K. and Valerian Lada-Mocarski.

REFERENCE: *La reliure originale française,* no. 12.

The Library of the Grolier Club of New York

ARMORIAL BINDINGS

It has ever been an observable custom for royal and wealthy bibliophiles to have their marks of ownership stamped on the covers of their books. This custom is variously responsible for a number of intriguing provenance puzzles, for the establishment of the provenance of many valuable items, and for the regrettable destruction of much bibliographic evidence when in later centuries collectors had entire libraries rebound and stamped with their arms.

The basic armorial style, which has survived through the centuries, is full undecorated leather with center arms or crest. An early example is the de Thou shown here, which has the coat of arms stamped in gold. However, the more frequent choice of the book collector has been to have his mark of ownership superimposed on the popular style of the day.

60. DANDINI ARMS   *ca. 1575*

Herodotus. *Historiographi libri VIIII.* Leiden, Seb. Gryphium, 1551.

Brown calf, gold-tooled. Plain endpapers; gilt edges. Double blue and white endbands; Greek style raised endcaps, smooth spine. 124 x 83 mm.

One of a large set of Greek works, now dispersed.

The arms of a prelate of the Dandini family are set in the central oval of a fanfare design. Two other bindings bearing these arms, each in a fanfare design, are known to exist and both are listed in the second edition of Hobson. One is on a 1566 Antwerp imprint, the other is on a 1576 Lyons imprint. Although Girolamo Dandino, the cardinal and diplomat, would be the obvious candidate, the date of his death, 1559, seems to preclude the possibility that these are from his collection. However, there was no other prelate of the Dandini family known to be living at this time.

The fanfare design, because of the central compartment which was frequently left undecorated, was particularly adaptable for armorial bindings. Several cardinals of the sixteenth and seventeenth centuries had fanfare bindings executed for them with their arms incorporated on the covers.

PROVENANCE: Earl of Hopetoun (Sotheby Sale, 25 February, 1889).

REFERENCE: Hobson, G. D., *Reliures à la fanfare* ed. 2.

Library of the Grolier Club of New York

61. ARMS OF JACQUES AUGUSTE DE THOU
1608-1617

Giovanni Pona. *Plantae seu simplicia ut vocant.* Basel, Sumptibus Lazari Zetzneri, 1608. Bound with: Nicolo Marogna. *Commentarius, in tractatus Dioscoridis, et Plini, de amomo.* Basel, Sumptibus Lazari Zetzneri, 1608; and Mathias de l'Obel. *Balsami, opobalsami, carpobalsami & xylobalsami.* London, execudebat Arnoldus Hatfield, impensis Johannis Norton, 1598.

Olive green morocco, gold-stamped arms on front and back covers. Gold-tooled cypher on spine. Plain endpapers. Double blue and pink silk endbands; five raised bands. 208 x 159 mm.

Jacques Auguste de Thou (1553-1617), historian, statesman and bibliophile of Renaissance France, inherited the core of his library from his uncle and his father, the latter's collection containing gifts of Jean Grolier. De Thou frequently had his books simply bound in plain leather or vellum with his arms stamped on the covers. A more elaborate style which he favored before his marriages was a fanfare design similar to that on the Dandini binding shown as figure 60.

De Thou is known to have had three sets of arms. His original arms as a bachelor were argent, a chevron between three gadflies sable. After his marriage to Marie Barbonçon, his arms incorporated hers. When he remarried after her death, his arms incorporated those of his second wife, Gasparde de la Chastre, as illustrated on this binding which also includes their cypher on the spine.

PROVENANCE: Bookplate of Musaeo Mouton-Fontenille Academiae Lugdunensis.

REFERENCES: Fletcher, *Bookbinding in England and France*, pp. 34-36, figs. 13, 15. Miner, *History of bookbinding*, p. 141.

Hunt Botanical Library

62. EVE STYLE   *ca. 1665-1715*

Dionys Joncquet. *Hortus regius*. Pars prior. Paris, Dionysius Langlois, 1665.

Tan morocco, gold-tooled, gold-stamped arms on front and back covers. Marbled endpapers; gilt edges over marble. Double pink and white endbands; six raised bands. 354 x 250 mm.

Dedication copy presented by the author to Louis XIV (1638-1715). The red numbered label of the royal library can be found on the tail of the spine and a crowned L stamped on p. 3. The arms of Louis XIV on the covers are those of France and Navarre, a style not frequently used by him.

The binding has been attributed to a pupil of Clovis Eve and its design, the semis of fleurs-de-lis with the arms center stamped, is very similar to those of bindings worked earlier by Eve for the royalty of France.

PROVENANCE: Contains the bookplates of the Earl of Aylesford, Packington and Warwick (hand-drawn), of Marjorie Post Davies, and of the Biblioteca Lamoniana.

REFERENCES: Olivier et al., *Manuel*, pls. 2493- 2494. *Hunt catalogue*, no. 298.

Hunt Botanical Library, from the original collection of Rachel McMasters Miller Hunt

63. ARMS OF BARON STUART DE ROTHESAY   *18th century*

Richard Bradley. *A general treatise of husbandry and gardening*. London, printed for J. Peele, 1724. Volume two of three.

Brown calf, sprinkled panels, blind tooling, blind-stamped arms on front and back covers. Plain endpapers; red sprinkled edges. Single red and white endbands; five raised bands, rebacked with sprinkled calf. 204 x 127 mm.

A utilitarian English calf binding of the first half of the eighteenth century, bearing the coronet and shield of the English diplomat, Charles Stuart (1779-1845), after 1828 Baron Stuart de Rothesay of the Isle of Bute. The baron left no male heir, so the peerage became extinct upon his death.

It appears that the baron had his arms stamped on the book after receiving it bound from a previous owner. This was not an uncommon practice.

PROVENANCE: Bookplates of Sir Cecill Wray of Lincolnshire (1734-1805) in each volume. Baron de Rothesay.

REFERENCES: Davenport, *English heraldic book-stamps*, pp. 357-358. *Hunt catalogue*, no. 459.

Hunt Botanical Library, from the original collection of Rachel McMasters Miller Hunt

64. FARAGHER AND LINDNER?   *ca. 1806-1817*

The country-man's recreation. London, printed by T. Mabb for William Shears, 1654.

Green straight-grain morocco, gold-tooled, gold-stamped crest on front and back covers. Purple endpapers and doublures; gilt and gauffered edges. Single green and white silk endbands; five raised double bands. 190 x 143 mm.

The coronets over the Spencer crest are those of a baron (left) and a marquis (right) and probably represent the two titles held by George Spencer, Baron Spencer of Wormleighton and Marquis of Blandford, before he became the 5th Duke of Marlborough in 1817. In 1806 he was given the title Baron Spencer and took a seat in the upper house. It was only in 1817 that he added Churchill to his name, by royal license.

The binding closely resembles the later work of Roger Payne, who had many imitators. It is possibly the work of Faragher and Lindner, who bound in the style of Payne and who are probably responsible for a similar binding for the Duke of Marlborough that was exhibited at the Walters Art Gallery in 1957 and bears the ducal crest.

PROVENANCE: Armorial bookplate of Johannes Georgius Home Drummond of Abbots Grange; bookseller's note on flyleaf: "from the Roxburgh Library."

REFERENCES: Miner, *History of bookbinding*, no. 540. *Burke's Peerage. Dictionary of national biography*, vol. XVIII. *Hunt catalogue*, no. 262.

Hunt Botanical Library, from the original collection of Rachel McMasters Miller Hunt

65. THOUVENIN   *ca. 1826-1830*

Luiz de Camoes. *I Lusiadi del Camoens*, [trans. by] A. Briccolani. Paris, Firmin Didot, 1826.

Green straight-grained morocco, gold- and blind-tooled, gold-stamped arms on front and back covers. Beige moiré silk endpapers and doublures; gilt edges. Single red and white silk endbands; four raised bands. 104 x 69 mm. Signed: Thouvenin

Arms of Louis-Philippe (1773-1850) as duc d'Orléans stamped in center of both covers. The crowned cypher of Louis-Philippe is tooled in gold on the spine above the binder's signature. Title page stamped with Bibliothèque du Roi, Neuilly.

Louis-Philippe was proclaimed King of France in 1830. He reigned until 1848 when the monarchy collapsed.

Joseph Thouvenin (1790-1834), known as Thouvenin l'aîné, was the most renowned of the brothers Thouvenin who bound in France during the years of the Restoration. Thouvenin, a pupil of the great Bozérian, is reputed to have restored the quality and art of bookbinding in France after it had deteriorated during the Revolution. While he is known for his cathedral bindings, he excelled in the restrospective genre—strictly imitative copies of the masters, whose work he surpassed. We have him to thank for naming the fanfare style when he bound *Fanfares et corvées abbadesques* for Charles Nodier, as well as for the establishment of the nineteenth century vogue for restrospective bindings.

A gentleman and equestrian, a perfectionist, a master of his trade who bound for the wealthy and royal French, Thouvenin signed his bindings simply "Thouvenin," or "R. P. Thouvenin," but the position of the signature on this volume emphasizes his own idea of his worth.

REFERENCES: Michon, *La reliure française*, pp. 119-121. Fletcher, *Bookbinding in England and France*, p. 76. Gruel, "Les Thouvenin, relieurs français au commencement du XIXe siècle," pp. 435-44. Olivier et al., *Manuel*, pl. 2577.

Hunt Library, from the original collection of Rachel McMasters Miller Hunt

66. ARMAND *ca. 1929*

Marianne Pelliot. *Verres anciens.* Paris & Brussels, Les editions G. Van Oest, 1929.

Gray morocco, recessed silver filagree panels, gold and blind tooling. Made endpapers of green and gold marbled paper and blue moiré silk, blue moiré silk doublures; top edge gilt. Double gray and yellow silk endbands; five raised bands. 333 x 262 mm. Signed: Armand

Number one of three deluxe copies on papier d'Arches à la cuve.

The arms, engraved with gold, are reputed to be those of Mme. Pelliot, on the upper cover, and of the sinologist M. Paul Pelliot, on the lower. The silver filagree panels are signed VB. Mme. Pelliot, who was the Countess Skoupenska before her marriage, presented this copy to her husband.

PROVENANCE: Purchased by the Corning Museum of Glass from the collection of Madame Pelliot.

The Corning Museum of Glass

67. AMERICAN HISTORICAL COMPANY *1965*

Thomas H. Bateman, comp. *DuPont and allied families, a genealogical study.* New York, The American Historical Company, 1965.

Blue morocco, red, green, turquoise, white morocco onlays, silver and gold tooling and stamping. Blue moiré silk endpapers, red leather doublures with white cloth onlays and gold stamping; gilt edges. Single yellow and gold false endbands; five false raised bands. 301 x 241 mm. Signed: The American Historical Company, Inc.

Arms of the duPont family on the upper cover; arms of Holcomb on the lower.

The American Historical Company, once the American Historical Society, published many of these genealogical records, bound in a similar manner or with simpler versions of the same style. The book used in the opening graphics of the Public Broadcasting System's "Once Upon a Classic" is another such example. That binding is on a copy of *Dow, Ball and allied families*, published in 1939 by the American Historical Society, and bears the arms of the Dow and the Ball families. The publishing house appears to be no longer in existence.

PROVENANCE: Presented to the Carnegie Library of Pittsburgh by Pierre S. duPont.

Pennsylvania Division, Carnegie Library of Pittsburgh

ARCHITECTURAL BINDINGS

Architectural elements such as columns, pilasters and archways have been used at times in binding design. Architectural bindings appeared with notable frequency in the fifteenth and sixteenth centuries and included a number done for the noted collectors Grolier and Mahieu. Although not exclusively applied to books of architecture, some of them did reproduce structures illustrated in the works themselves. However, these cover designs may have more of a relationship to the elaborately decorative architectural title page borders of the sixteenth century than to any tendency to illustrate the text. Stamped cathedral bindings, popular in the nineteenth century, may be considered a manifestation of this style. The architectural analogy of the binding as the door to the content of the book has been utilized by several modern binders.

68. FRENCH ARCHITECTURAL BINDING *ca. 1554*

Photograph of binding on: Herodian. *L'histoire . . . translatee de Greq en Francoys par Jacques des Contes de Vintemille.* Lyons, Guillaume Rouillé, 1554.

Golden brown morocco, gold-tooled. Gilt edges. Two pairs of green silk ties.

A superb example of a mid-sixteenth century French architectural binding, whose design may be related to the architectural title page border of the book. Both border and binding include a design of bows and arrows, which may refer to Diane de Poitiers. Paul Needham points out that the pattern of compartments and strapwork on the entablature of this binding is similar to that found later in Parisian fanfare bindings.

REFERENCE: Needham, *Twelve centuries,* no. 69.

The Pierpont Morgan Library, New York

69. ARCHITECTURAL TITLE PAGE BORDER *1611*

Jean Théodore de Bry. *Florilegium novum.* Oppenheim, a Iohanne Theodoro de Bry, 1611.

An engraved title page, providing an inviting view into the garden from the portico.

REFERENCE: *Hunt catalogue,* no. 190.

Hunt Botanical Library, from the original collection of Rachel McMasters Miller Hunt

70. RACHEL McMASTERS MILLER HUNT *1916*

Samuel Rogers. *Italy.* London, Cadell and Moxon, 1836.

Rose levant morocco, gold-tooled. Rose moiré silk endpapers and doublures; gilt and gauffered edges. Double pink and green silk endbands; projecting endcaps, five raised bands. 205 x 135 mm. Signed: [lamb] R Mc M M, 1916

This is an architectural binding in the Italian portico style with two pilasters and is identical to the binding presented by Mrs. Hunt to the British Museum in 1962 at the suggestion of Howard Nixon.

REFERENCE: Titcombe, *Bookbinding career,* no. 105.

Hunt Library

71. JEAN GUNNER *1979*

Stow: the gardens of the right honorable the Lord Viscount Cobham. London, printed by B. Seeley and sold by John and James Rivington and Robert Sayer, 1749.

Dark brown calf, black and tan onlays and inlays, black

paint, gold and blind tooling. Marbled endpapers; original red sprinkled edges. Single red and white silk endbands; five raised bands. 204 x 135 mm. Signed: J. Gunner 1979

The gardens at Stowe, the seat of Richard Temple, Viscount Cobham, were the subject of many guide books which reproduced notable architectural embellishments of the landscape, including the Temple of British Worthies. This binding illustrates one of the buildings figured in the text, there labelled "Two pavilions at the entrance to the Park."

Hunt Botanical Library, from the original collection of Rachel McMasters Miller Hunt

PICTORIAL BINDINGS

The tradition of the binder as illustrator is a long one, albeit sporadic. One well-known sixteenth century example is on an arithmetic, De arte supputandi *by Cuthbert Tunstall, exhibited at the Walters Art Gallery in 1957. On the upper cover of this calf binding are painted the personifications of Astrology, Music Geometry and Arithmetic.[1] Two centuries later, the predilection for the colorful and novel was gratified by the painted vellum bindings of Edwards of Halifax. However, the pictorial designs on these eighteenth century bindings did not necessarily relate to the text within.*

The application of color-printing to binding materials allowed artists in the nineteenth century to extend their illustrations of the text onto the covers of the books. In the twentieth century, greater flexibility has been achieved through the availability of new materials and the innovative use of leathers; with that, surface illustration frequently becomes expressive design.

---

[1]Miner, *History of bookbinding*, no. 344.

72. EDWARDS OF HALIFAX *ca. 1780*

George Ballard. *Memoirs of several ladies of Great Britain, who have been celebrated for their writings or skill in the learned languages, arts and sciences.* Oxford, printed by W. Jackson for the author, 1752.

Vellum, gold-tooled and painted with vignette in color on upper cover and monochrome portrait on lower cover. Marbled endpapers; gilt edges. Single pink and beige silk endbands, smooth spine. 269 x 216 mm.

Edwards of Halifax was a family book-selling and binding firm noted for its painted vellum bindings. A process was patented by a son, James, in 1785 by which vellum was made transparent when soaked in a solution of pearl ash. A drawing or painting executed on the underside would then be visible yet protected.

Many armorial bindings were produced by the firm in this manner. Classical and biblical scenes, most frequently in monochrome, were also popular. On occasion the Halifax bindings illustrated the text, as on a copy of *The father's revenge,* or as with the portraits on a copy of the biographies of Lord Herbert of Cherbury and Comte de Grammont. The binding exhibited here is particularly notable for the use of color in the vignette on the upper cover.

REFERENCES: Nixon, *Broxbourne,* no. 93; *Five centuries,* p. 174; "English bookbindings LXXXI." Chas. J. Sawyer, *Catalogue 273,* no. 37.

Hunt Library, from the original collection of Rachel McMasters Miller Hunt

73. KELLIEGRAM *19th century*

Augustus Septimus and Henry Mayhew. *The greatest plague of life: or The adventures of a lady in search of a good servant, by one who has been "almost worried to death."* Illustrated by George Cruikshank. London, David Bogue, 1847.

Red morocco, blue, black, beige, gray and brown morocco onlays, gold and blind tooling. Green moiré silk endpapers and doublures; gilt edges. Double red, green and gold silk endbands; five raised bands. 183 x 128 mm. Signed: Kelliegram Binding

Center vignette on upper cover after George Cruikshank's illustration in the text entitled "The Sentimental Novel Reader."

PROVENANCE: Presented to Hunt Library by Mrs. Charles L. Snowdon, Jr.

Hunt Library

74. SANGORSKI AND SUTCLIFFE *1912*

Rubáiyát of Omar Khayyám. London, Bernard Quaritch, 1872.

Blue morocco, red, green and dark blue morocco onlays, gold tooling, 14 sapphire and 13 garnet insets. Front cover has recessed oval with multicolored painted snake and apples in relief; lower cover has recessed quatrefoil. Made endpapers of gold-tooled brown levant and brown silk; brown levant doublures with blue, green and red inlays, gold tooling; top edge gilt. Double brown, blue and beige silk endbands; five raised bands. 210 x 160 mm. Signed: 1912 Designed by F. Sangorski   Front doublure signed: R. D. no. 603202   Bound by Sangorski & Sutcliffe London.

The luxurious theme and sensual extravagance of the *Rubáiyát of Omar Khayyám* fascinated the designer, Francis Sangorski, inspiring him to bindings of great opulence. The firm produced many bindings for this work, often using peacock or grapevine motifs. The most elaborate was the "Great Omar," which contained 1,050 jewels set amongst colorful inlays and heavy gold tooling. This extraordinary work exists now only in photographs as the original went down with the *Titanic* and a later copy was destroyed during World War II.

PROVENANCE: Maurice Inman (Sale 1951). Bookplate of the Family of Henry Posner.

REFERENCES: Stonehouse, *The great Omar.* Middleton, *English craft bookbinding,* pp. 125-126. Elkind, "Jewelled bindings," pp. 403-405.

From the collection established in memory of Henry Posner

75. RIVIÈRE & SON *1935*

The Holy Bible containing the old and new testaments: translated out of the original tongues and with the former translations diligently compared and revised by His Majesty's special command; appointed to be read in churches. Oxford, printed at the University Press, 1935. Volume one of two.

Red levant morocco, gold- and blind-tooled. Plain endpapers and doublures; gilt edges. Double light and dark red silk endbands. Five raised bands. 453 x 346 mm. Signed: Bound by Riviere & Son, London

Oxford Lectern Bible, one of 200 copies designed by Bruce Rogers. Binding designed by Lynton Lamb.

The Bible is frequently bound using designs which reflect its content. The binding shown here is an example of expressive design, with the dove, cross and orb signifying the power of the word of God.

Buffalo and Erie County Public Library, Rare Book Room

76. THOMAS W. PATTERSON   1956

Hugh Cleland. *George Washington in the Ohio Valley.* Pittsburgh, University of Pittsburgh, 1955.

Brown oasis morocco, gold- and blind-tooled. Striped blue and beige endpapers and doublures; top edge gilt. Double black, gray and white silk endbands; five raised bands. 233 x 159 mm. Binder's ticket: Thos. Patterson Bookbinding   Crafton, Penna.

The outline on the upper cover is of the original sites of Forts Pitt and Duquesne at "The Point"—the jut of land at the confluence of the Allegheny and Monongahela Rivers. George Washington was a member of the French and Indian War expedition that recaptured Fort Duquesne, thereafter named Fort Pitt.

PROVENANCE: Given to the Historical Society of Western Pennsylvania by Miss Jeannette Seneff.

REFERENCES: *Thomas W. Patterson, bookbinder,* no. 29. Guild of Book Workers, *Exhibition.*

Historical Society of Western Pennsylvania

77. PHILIP SMITH   1974-1975

William Shakespeare. *The tragedie of Hamlet Prince of Denmarke. Illustrated by Edward Gordon Craig.* Weimar, Cranach Press, 1930.

Black and gray oasis morocco, multicolored feathered onlays and maril. Plum colored endpapers, purple suede doublures; gilt edges. Double multicolor silk endbands; smooth spine. 353 x 235 mm. Binder's ticket: Philip Smith April 1975

COLOPHON: This is copy number A [of seven copies on vellum].

This copy includes three extra sets of proofs signed by the artist.

"The Hamlet originated as a painted sketch and is interpreted in a collage of leather fragments."—Philip Smith.

REFERENCES: Lilly Library, *British bookbinding today,* no. 35. Smith, "Designing for bookbinders-pt. 2," p. 14.

Lilly Library, Indiana University, Bloomington, Indiana

78. GÉRARD CHARRIERE   1977

Jean Cocteau. *La voix humaine.* Paris, Librarie Stock, Delamain et Boutelleau, 1930.

Green morocco, black and white onlays, gold tooling. Cream suede endpapers and doublures; top edge gilt. Single red and green endbands; smooth spine. 182 x 121 mm. Signed: Gérard Charriere

Gérard Charriere, born in 1935, studied bookbinding at Ecole des Arts et Metiers in Basel for three years and at Ecole Estienne in Paris for two years. Coming to the United States in 1964, he worked at the Newberry Library restoring its books and manuscripts until 1968. He then moved to New York where he has established his own studio for the rebinding and restoration of books. He teaches private classes in fine binding, tooling and restoration, and lectures extensively on these subjects. Studying painting at the Art Students League in New York, he exhibits his paintings and bindings together.

John M. Wing Foundation, the Newberry Library

79. BERNARD C. MIDDLETON   1977

Bernard C. Middleton. *A history of English craft bookbinding technique.* London, Hafner, 1963.

Tan oasis, brown and black inlays, gold and black tooling. Jap endpapers and doublures; gilt edges. Double four-colored endbands; smooth spine. 235 x 155 mm. Signed: M [monogram] 1977

The design suggests a lying press and the screw of a standing press.

REFERENCE: *Designer bookbinders 3,* p. 28.

Frank Buxton

80. JEAN GUNNER   1979

Francis Bacon. *Of gardens.* Chelsea on Thames, Swan Press, 1928.

Dark green oasis, light blue, gray and purple oasis inlays, gray, purple, red, and shades of green oasis and toned vellum onlays, gold and black tooling. Japanese paper endpapers and doublures; top edge gilt. Single purple and green silk endbands; smooth spine. 291 x 232 mm. Signed: J. Gunner 1979

Number 69 of 100 copies.

The design of the binding echoes the architectural elements found in the title pages of Bacon's time, but the vibrantly colored leathers give a photographic effect.

Hunt Botanical Library, from the original collection of Rachel McMasters Miller Hunt

THE MODERN MOVEMENT

What is now called the modern movement in bookbinding was prefigured in the philosophies of H. Marius-Michel in France and T. J. Cobden-Sanderson in England, and realized in the work of Pierre Legrain and Edgar Mansfield. Legrain and Mansfield broke away dramatically from the traditional and decorative designs of the past and applied the abstract aesthetics of the modern movement in art to bookbinding design. This new direction has been characterized by the asymmetrical treatment of rectangular space, the use of expressive, non-figurative designs, and the innovative use of color, leather and synthetic materials.

That the binder is a creative artist is a central tenet of the modern movement; it is what Edgar Mansfield considers to be his "primary contribution to bookbinding . . . to bring the philosophy and experience of a creative artist to the technique of the craft, and add one new dimension—the active interplay between expressive creative design, and potentially creative and expressive techniques and media."

81. HENRI MARIUS-MICHEL   *ca. 1906-1925*

Albert Victor Samain. *Aux flancs du vase. Ouvrage orné de compositions executées et gravées par Gaston La Touche.* Paris, imprimé pour la Société du Livre d' Art, 1906.

Dark brown crushed levant morocco, shades of tan and brown morocco onlays, blind tooling. Tan morocco doublures, with brown, green and purple morocco onlays, gold and blind tooling. Made endpapers of muted red and green silk, and red, brown and green marbled paper; gilt edges. Double yellow, red and olive green silk endbands; four raised bands. 249 x 187 mm. Signed: Marius Michel.

Number 91 of 100 copies, including a set of artist's proofs.

A binding in the naturalistic floral style for which Henri Marius-Michel was best known.

Henri Marius-Michel (1846-1925) was the son of the great gilder, Marius-Michel, who worked for Gruel and Capé. With his father he wrote *La reliure française,* 1880 and *L'ornamentation des reliures modernes,* 1889. Marius-Michel believed that the color of the leather and the design should reflect the nature or tone of the book, that an old book should be bound in a style reflective of its age, and that a new book should have a modern binding. For a Marius-Michel binding which reflects the period of the book, yet retains the personality of the binder, see Plate I in *Masterpieces of French modern bindings.*

PROVENANCE: Bookplate of R. Descamps Scrive; gift of Frank Altschul.

REFERENCES: Prideaux, *Bookbinders and their craft,* pp. 126-128. Michon, *La reliure française,* pp. 127-129. *Masterpieces of French modern bindings,* pp. iv-vii. Roylance, "The Altschul Collection," p. 64.

The Beinecke Rare Book and Manuscript Library, Yale University

82. PIERRE LEGRAIN   *ca. 1919*

Examples of modern bookbinding designed and executed by Robt. Rivière & Son. London, Bernard Quaritch, 1919.

Dark tan morocco, green, light and dark brown morocco onlays, blind, gold and palladium tooling. Blue suede endleaves and doublures. Double turquoise and beige endbands; smooth spine. 290 x 237 mm. Signed: Pierre Legrain

Pierre Legrain (1888-1929), decorator and ensemblier, revolutionized the art of bookbinding by going beyond surface decoration to expressive design, intimately unifying the text and cover. As equally revolutionary was his extension of the design across the spine, from cover to cover. He knew his materials well and exploited the color and textures of leather to express in modern aesthetic terms the essence of the book. When appropriate, Legrain took inspiration from historic designs. For a binding on *La Leçon d'amour dans un parc,* a novel in the eighteenth century manner, Legrain worked eighteenth century dentelle borders in twentieth century patterns.

REFERENCES: Miner, *History of bookbinding,* pp. 247-249. *Masterpieces of French modern bindings,* no. 14, pl. IV.

John M. Wing Foundation, the Newberry Library

83. ROSE ADLER   *1931*

Tristan Bernard. *Tableau de la boxe.* Paris, Éditions de la nouvelle revue française, 1922.

Polished rust calf, diced tan and dark blue calf inlays, red calf onlays, gold and blind tooling. Made endpapers of rust moiré silk and marbled paper; doublures of diced tan calf, red calf onlays with blue calf inlays and gold tooling. Double orange, rust and brown silk endbands; smooth spine. 245 x 200 mm. Signed: Rose 1931 Adler   A. Jeanne   Dor

Rose Adler (1890-1959) studied binding under Andrée Langrand at the Ecole d'Art Décoratif and finishing at Noulhac's. She began binding in the early twenties as a disciple of Pierre Legrain and did many volumes for Jacques Doucet, the "couturier et collectionneur éclectique" who encouraged Pierre Legrain in his craft. Unlike many French designers, Rose Adler was responsible for the forwarding and finishing of most of her books until her later years. She was a founding member of the Société de la Reliure Originale.

Spencer Collection, The New York Public Library, Astor, Lenox and Tilden Foundations

84. PAUL BONET   *1964*

Camille Bryen. *Désécriture.* Alés, P.A.B., 1962.

Black and white box calf, shades of yellow, red, green and brown calf onlays, blind tooling. Black and white suede endpapers edged with green calf; gilt edges. Double white silk headband, double black silk tailband; smooth spine. 129 x 326 mm. Signed: Paul Bonet   Dated: 1964

Copy number V of 10 with the etching on three different papers, of a total edition of 50. Etchings signed by the author.

Paul Bonet (1888-1971) was a skilled artisan and designer with an unusually diverse imagination. He was greatly influenced by the skill of Legrain but his designs were always his own. He was particularly inspired by modern illustrated books, especially the work of Picasso. Bonet was not a specialist in any artistic style; he experimented with them all, as well as with textures, color, shapes, typography, and palladium and gold tooling. His first profession was fashion design and for a time he practiced both simultaneously. Eventually binding design involved him totally and in 1946 he brought together French binders in the Société de la Reliure Originale.

PROVENANCE: Bookplate of J. R. Abbey (Sotheby sale, 2 June 1970, no. 2551). Bought for the Royal Library by the Foundation of Friends of the Library.

REFERENCES: *Verslag omtrent de Koninklijke Bibliotheek,* pp. 24-25. *Modern British and French bookbindings from the collection of J. R. Abbey,* no. 94.

Royal Library, The Hague, The Netherlands

85. ALFRED DE SAUTY   *ca. 1926*

Geoffrey Chaucer [supposed author]. *The floure and the leafe, & The boke of Cupide, god of love, or The cuckow and the nightingale.* Hammersmith, Kelmscott Press, 1896.

Black levant morocco, multicolored niger onlays, gold

tooling. Black endpapers, black levant morocco doublures framed by bands of green niger with repeat of onlaid floral design of covers; top edge gilt. Purple and white silk endbands; five raised bands. 236 x 163 mm. Signed: Donnelley — Chicago

Designed by Alfred de Sauty and probably finished by Leonard Mounteney just before he left for the Cuneo Press, this binding is not typical of the earlier work of de Sauty, which had a strong art nouveau flavor.

Alfred de Sauty (1870-1949), etcher and bookbinder, worked as an electrician for the Eastern Telegraph Company before going to Rivière's as a finisher in the 1890s. He soon established a reputation as an excellent craftsman and taught bookbinding at the Central School of Arts and Crafts in London between 1903 and 1914. In 1923 de Sauty left England to become head of the Extra Bindery at the Lakeside Press in Chicago, where he was responsible for the design of bindings until 1935.

REFERENCES: For an interesting comparison with de Sauty's earlier work, see Nixon, "English bookbindings XVIII," and *Five centuries*, no. 97.

Binding and information on de Sauty courtesy of the Graphic Conservation Department, R. R. Donnelley & Sons Company

86. ALFRED DE SAUTY   *1930*

Edgar Allen Poe. *Tales, illustrated by W. A. Dwiggins.* Chicago, The Lakeside Press, 1930.

Black levant morocco, red niger onlays, blind tooling. Bright red endpapers; polished black-dyed top edge. Single black and white silk endbands; five raised bands. 194 x 130 mm. Signed: Donnelley — Chicago

The Graphic Conservation Department, R. R. Donnelley & Sons Company

87. TREVOR JONES   *1976*

Nikolai Gogol. *The overcoat.* Verona, Officina Bodoni, 1975.

Toned calf vellum, morocco, pigskin, fur and plastic onlays, aniline dye. Made endpapers and doublures of marbled paper and unbleached linen; top edge gilt. Gray and white linen endbands; smooth spine. 305 x 210 mm. Signed: TRJ · 76 Trevor Jones-1976-

Shown with its cloth box, belted and buttoned.

Born in 1931, Trevor Jones studied illustration at the Harrow School of Art, and bookbinding with Arthur Johnson at the Hornsey College of Art. Currently, he is head of the Arts and Crafts Department at the amalgamated St. John's and Ripon Colleges where he is responsible for design and publicity. Known for his use of unusual materials in binding, he has recently been experimenting with stencils and aniline dyes.

PROVENANCE: Commissioned by K. D. Duval.

Kulgin Duval and Colin Hamilton

88. GEORGES LEROUX   *1964*

André Du Bouchet. *L'avril.* Paris, pour Janine Hao, 1963.

Polished tan calf, dark red, orange, purple, red and green polished calf onlays. Cream suede endpapers and doublures; top edge gilt. Double green silk endbands; smooth spine. 127 x 171 mm. Signed: Leroux   Dated: 1964

Number 3 of first 10 copies, of a total edition of 60, signed by author and illustrator. Includes five original etchings by Gaston-Louis Roux.

Georges Leroux, born in 1922, practiced bookbinding with his wife in a bookshop in Cannes which they opened in 1946. He moved to Paris in 1956 where, dedicated to binding, he specializes in working with avant-garde publications.

REFERENCE: *Modern British and French bookbindings from the collection of J. R. Abbey.*

John M. Wing Foundation, The Newberry Library

89. EDGAR MANSFIELD   *1937*

Herman Broch. *The sleepwalkers.* London, Martin Secker, 1932.

Crimson crushed morocco, gold-tooled. Plain endpapers; top edge gilt. Orange and green silk endbands; five raised bands. 214 x 137 mm.

Edgar Mansfield was born in London in 1907, and emigrated in 1912 to New Zealand where he received his early art training. He studied bookbinding in London under William Matthews at the Central School of Arts and Crafts, and design under Elsa Taterka at The Reimann School. Well known also as a sculptor, Edgar Mansfield now has retired from bookbinding and lives in New Zealand practicing other art forms. In the Queen's 1979 Birthday Honors List he was awarded the Order of the British Empire for his services to bookbinding and sculpture.

Edgar Mansfield set out not to decorate the book, but to create a piece of art that would be an integral part of the work it enclosed. His early work provoked extreme reaction and he was accused of "the rape of the book" and of "destroying all tradition." But opinion changed greatly and Howard Nixon commented in 1966, "Much that is new in modern British bookbinding is unquestionably due to Edgar Mansfield's example and teaching."

REFERENCES: Mansfield, *Modern design in bookbinding*, pp. 7, 19. Lilly Library, *British bookbinding today*, pp. 38-40.

David H. H. and Claire S. Felix

90. EDGAR MANSFIELD   *1964*

Prosper Merimee. *Carmen. With 38 illustrations engraved by Picasso.* Paris, La Bibliothèque Française, 1949.

Crimson red native-dyed morocco, black and natural recessed onlays, blind tooling. Endpapers colored by binder; top edge gilt. Black silk endbands; smooth spine. 340 x 260 mm. Signed: Edgar Mansfield

Number 1 of 309 copies signed by Picasso.

Shown with tooling patterns and sketches.

REFERENCES: Lilly Library, *British bookbinding today*, no. 22. Mansfield, *Modern design in bookbinding*, p. 92.

Lilly Library, Indiana University, Bloomington, Indiana; patterns and sketches lent by K. D. Duval

91. WILLIAM MATTHEWS *1975*

Longus. *Daphnis and Chloe. A most sweet and pleasant pastoral romance for young ladies, translated out of the Greek by Geo. Thornley.* London, A. Zwemmer, 1937.

Green oasis, gold-tooled. Handmade cloudy endpapers; edges uncut. Pink silk endbands; four raised bands. 135 x 203 mm. Signed: 19 W. Matthews 75

One of 50 copies with duplicate set of the woodcuts by Maillol, printed in bistre.

According to Bernard Middleton, William Matthews (1898-1977) was "one of the finest craftsmen this century has produced. But more than that, he linked the past securely to the future by teaching his considerable skills to a large proportion of the next generation of English bookbinders." Beginning his studies in bookbinding at the age of 13 at the Central School of Arts and Crafts, he later was apprenticed as a finisher at W. T. Morrell's bindery. In 1926 he founded his own firm where he worked singlehandedly until his death. Also at that time he embarked on his long teaching career. His students included Edgar Mansfield, Bernard Middleton, Roger Powell and Peter Waters. His love of gold tooling is very evident on his bindings, which catch and reflect the light giving the "solid brilliance of deep gold." He was awarded the insignia of the City and Guilds Institute of London, their highest honor and the first time it had been given to a bookbinder, just before his death.

REFERENCES: Victoria & Albert Museum, *Two modern binders,* p. [1]. Lilly Library, *British bookbinding today,* no. 25. Harrop, "Craft binders at work I."

Lilly Library, Indiana University, Bloomington, Indiana

92. ROGER POWELL *1963*

William Shakespeare. *The tragedie of Hamlet Prince of Denmarke. Illustrated by Edward Gordon Craig.* Weimar, Cranach Press, 1930.

Black morocco, blue and purple onlays, gold and blind tooling. Grey paper endpapers and doublures. Single purple, green and cream endbands; smooth spine, one raised band. 355 x 242 mm. Signed: Roger [monogram] 1963 Powell

Colophon: This is a copy A [of seven copies on vellum].

This copy includes three extra sets of proofs signed by the artist.

Roger Powell, born in 1896, comes from a family of craftsmen influenced by William Morris and the Arts and Crafts movement. Howard Nixon says that, on Powell's demobilization from the Royal Flying Corps, "he showed an untypical lack of originality in taking to poultry farming in partnership with his brother. He claims to have made more or less indestructible poultry houses but no living." Powell started bookbinding seriously in 1930 at the Central School of Arts and Crafts, London, where his teachers included Douglas Cockerell. He was also in charge of bookbinding instruction at the Royal College of Art from 1943 to 1956. The repair and rebinding of early books and research on their structures are his main interests. He is perhaps best known for his rebinding of manuscripts on vellum, including the *Book of Kells*. In 1976 he received the Order of the British Empire for his contribution to the preservation of books.

PROVENANCE: Bookplate of J. R. Abbey.

REFERENCES: Nixon, *Roger Powell & Peter Waters,* p. 1. *Modern British and French bindings from the collection of J. R. Abbey,* no. 45. Harrop, "Craft binders at work III."

Bought on the Pocahontas Press Fund for the John M. Wing Foundation, the Newberry Library

93. SYBIL PYE *1939*

Robert Bridges. *The testament of beauty.* Oxford, at the Clarendon Press, 1929.

Dark green morocco, natural, tan and rust calf inlays, gold tooling. Plain endpapers; dark green morocco doublures, natural, tan and rust calf inlays. Single red silk endbands; five raised bands. 295 x 225 mm. Signed: . MCM: XXX IX .   :SP[monogram]:

Self-taught, using Douglas Cockerell's *Bookbinding and the care of books,* Sybil Pye (d. ca. 1957) began binding in 1906. She is well known for her distinctive inlay work and cubist designs. Her earlier work is readily identified by its vivid colors, including orange, red, purple and green. She was greatly influenced by the work of Charles Ricketts, whose tools she used in addition to those which he cut especially for her.

PROVENANCE: Bookplate of J. R. Abbey.

Spencer Collection, The New York Public Library, Astor, Lenox and Tilden Foundations

94. IVOR ROBINSON *1971-1972*

The song of Solomon. Guildford, Surrey, printed by Ronald King for Circle Press Publications, 1968.

Black oasis, gray, red and blue oasis, black and white calf onlays, gold tooling. Navy blue suede endpapers, brown suede doublures; rough gilt edges. Double white, gold, gray and black silk endbands; smooth spine. 390 x 290 mm. Signed: Ivor Robinson 1972

Number 25 of an edition of 150.

Shown with working drawings.

Ivor Robinson, born in 1924, began as an apprentice in a miscellaneous bindery and later studied under Eric Burdett at Bournemouth College of Art. He now works at his bindery in Oxford and is senior lecturer in bookbinding and visual studies at Oxford Polytechnic. Currently he is working on an extended version of his *Introducing bookbinding,* which was first published in 1968. A superb craftsman and an artist with a unique freedom in his designs, Ivor Robinson has made his mark on twentieth century binding design through his linear variations.

"I am primarily interested in drawing—hence the linear quality of my work. In respect of the book cover, I am principally interested in determining and defining areas of activity, areas of space, and points of emphasis. In matters of technique I am a traditionalist, and in design attitudes and preferences I am probably a classicist."—I. Robinson

From the collection of Maggy Magerstadt Rosner; drawings lent by binder.

59

95. IVOR ROBINSON   *1975*

*The four gospels of the Lord Jesus Christ, according to the
authorized version of King James I with decorations by Eric Gill.*
London, Golden Cockerell Press, 1931.

Black cape goatskin, black oasis inlays, black and white
calf onlays, palladium tooling. Purple suede endpapers,
charcoal suede doublures; rough palladium edges. Double
endbands with leather centers; smooth spine. 340 x 250 mm.
Signed: 19 · IR · 75

Shown with working drawings.

Bridwell Library, Southern Methodist University; drawings lent by binder.

60

96. PHILIP SMITH   *1967-1968*

William Shakespeare. *King Lear, with lithographs by Oskar
Kokoschka.* London, Ganymed Original Editions Limited,
1963.

Purple oasis morocco and orange cape morocco, multicolored feathered onlays. Oatmeal endpapers, purple suede
doublures; gilt edges. Double multicolored silk endbands;
smooth spine. 457 x 362 mm. Binder's ticket: Philip Smith

Of Philip Smith, born in 1928, Edgar Mansfield has said
that he "brings to bookbinding one of the most original
minds ever to add technical mastery to design competence:
his parallel training and experience as a painter is of equal
significance in bringing to bookbinding the mind of an
artist." First studying bookbinding at the Southport School
of Art and later under Roger Powell at the Royal College
of Art, Smith established his own workshop in 1961. Since
then he has experimented with new binding structures,
display techniques and, most notably, feathered onlays and
'maril,' which may stand for *ma*rbled *i*nlaid *l*eather. He has
lectured and written extensively on his approach to the art
and craft of bookbinding; his *New directions in bookbinding*
was published in 1974.

PROVENANCE: Colin Franklin, originally bound for Anthony
Fair.

REFERENCES: Smith, *The Lord of the rings and other bindings
of P. Smith; New directions in bookbinding,* pp. 8, 30-31, pl. 21.

Mr. and Mrs. Arnold Elkind

ADAMS, FREDERICK B. *Bookbindings by T. J. Cobden-Sanderson; an exhibition at the Pierpont Morgan Library* . . . New York, 1969.

AUSTIN, GABRIEL. *The library of Jean Grolier; a preliminary catalogue.* New York, 1971.

(Brown University Library.) *William Morris and the Kelmscott Press; an exhibition* . . . Providence, 1960.

(Buffalo Fine Arts Academy.) *Catalog of an exhibition of bookbinding representing the work of twenty-five years by John F. Grabau* . . . Buffalo, 1930.

CHAS. J. SAWYER. *Fine bindings.* Catalogue 273. London, 1967.

COBDEN-SANDERSON, THOMAS J. "Bookbinding." *English illustrated magazine,* vol. 8, 1890.

———. *The journals of Thomas James Cobden-Sanderson, 1879-1922.* 2 vols. London, 1926.

DAVENPORT, CYRIL. *English heraldic book-stamps.* London, 1909.

Designer bookbinders; an illustrated directory of fellows, 3. 1978.

DROUOT RIVE GAUCHE. *Importants livres illustrés et oeuvres originales d'artistes modernes, gouaches, dessins, gravures.* Paris, 1978.

ELKIND, M. WIEDER. "Jeweled bindings, 1900-39." *The book collector,* vol. 24, no. 3, Autumn 1975.

FLETCHER, WILLIAM Y. *Bookbinding in England and France.* London, 1897.

GRUEL, LÉON. "Les Thouvenin relieurs français au commencement du XIXe siècle." *Bulletin du bibliophile et du bibliothécaire,* 1898.

(The Guild of Book Workers.) *An exhibition of hand bookbinding, case-making, restoration, calligraphy & illumination, and hand-decorated papers* . . . New York, 1959.

HAEBLER, KONRAD. *Rollen- und Plattenstempel des XVI. Jahrhunderts, unter Mitwirkung von Dr. Ilse Schunke.* 2 vols. Leipzig, 1928-29.

Hand bookbinding today, an international art; an exhibition organized by the San Francisco Museum of Modern Art in cooperation with The Hand Bookbinders of California. San Francisco, 1978.

HARROP, DOROTHY A. "Craft binders at work I: William F. Matthews." *The book collector,* vol. 21, no. 4, Winter 1972.

———. "Craft binders at work III: Roger Powell." *The book collector,* vol. 22, no. 4, Winter 1973.

———. "Craft binders at work IV: Sydney Morris Cockerell." *The book collector,* vol. 23, no. 2, Summer 1974.

———. "Craft binders at work VIII: Bernard Chester Middleton." *The book collector,* vol. 26, no. 3, Autumn 1977.

HARTHAN, JOHN P. *Bookbindings.* 2nd rev. ed. Victoria & Albert Museum, 1961.

HOBSON, ANTHONY R. A. *French and Italian collectors and their bindings, illustrated from examples in the library of J. R. Abbey.* Oxford, 1953.

HOBSON, GEOFFREY D. *Bindings in Cambridge libraries.* Cambridge, 1929.

———. *English bindings, 1490-1940, in the library of J. R. Abbey.* London, 1940.

———. *Les reliures à la fanfare. Le problème de l'S fermé.* London, 1935.

———. *Les reliures à la fanfare. Le problème de l'S fermé.* 2. ed., augm. d'un supplément contenant des additions et corrections par Anthony R. A. Hobson. Amsterdam, 1970.

(Hunt, Rachel McM. M.) *Catalogue of botanical books in the collection of* . . . Compiled by Jane Quinby and Allan Stevenson. 2 vols. in 3. Pittsburgh, 1958-1961.

LE ROUX DE LINCY, ANTOINE JEAN VICTOR. *Recherches sur Jean Grolier, sur sa vie et sa bibliothèque, suivies d'un catalogue des livres qui lui ont appartenu.* 2 vols. Paris, 1866.

(Lilly Library.) *British bookbinding today, with an introduction by Edgar Mansfield.* 1976.

MAGGS BROTHERS. *Book bindings: historical & decorative.* [Catalogue] no. 407. London, 1921.

———. *Book bindings: historical & decorative.* [Catalogue] no. 489. London, 1927.

———. *Bookbinding in Great Britain, sixteenth to the twentieth century.* Catalogue 966. London, 1975.

MANSFIELD, EDGAR. *Modern design in bookbinding; the work of Edgar Mansfield.* Boston, 1966.

Masterpieces of French modern bindings. New York, 1947.

MICHON, LOUIS-MARIE. *La reliure française.* Paris, 1951.

———. *Les reliures mosaïquées du XVIIIe siècle.* Paris, 1956.

MIDDLETON, BERNARD C. *A history of English craft bookbinding technique.* New York and London, 1963.

[Miner, Dorothy.] *The history of bookbinding, 525-1950 A.D.; an exhibition* . . . *organized by the Walters Art Gallery* and presented in cooperation with *The Baltimore Museum of Art*. Baltimore, 1957.

Modern British and French bookbindings from the collection of J. R. Abbey; [an exhibition organized by the] Arts Council. Introductions by Howard M. Nixon. London, 1965.

(Morgan, J. Pierpont.) *Catalogue of a collection of books formed by James Toovey principally from the library of the Earl of Gosford, the property of J. Pierpont Morgan*. New York, 1901.

NEEDHAM, PAUL. *Twelve centuries of bookbinding, 400-1600*. New York, 1979.

———. *William Morris and the art of the book; with essays on William Morris, as book collector by Paul Needham, as calligrapher by Joseph Dunlap, and as typographer by John Dreyfus*. New York, 1976.

NIXON, HOWARD M. *Broxbourne Library: styles and designs of bookbindings from the twelfth to the twentieth century*. London, 1956.

———. "English bookbindings XVIII: a mosaic binding by A. de Sauty, c. 1904." *The book collector*, vol. 5, no. 3, Autumn 1956.

———. "English bookbindings XLV: an Eton binding by Roger Payne, 1764." *The book collector*, vol. 12, no. 2, Summer 1963.

———. "English bookbindings LXXIX: a London binding by Rivière & Son, c. 1905." *The book collector*, vol. 20, no. 4, Winter 1971.

———. "English bookbindings LXXXI: a signed Edwards of Halifax binding, c. 1782." *The book collector*, vol. 21, no. 2, Summer 1972.

———. *English Restoration bookbindings: Samuel Mearne and his contemporaries*. London, 1974.

———. *Five centuries of English bookbinding*. London, 1978.

———. *Roger Powell & Peter Waters*. 1965.

———. *Sixteenth-century gold-tooled bookbindings in the Pierpont Morgan Library*. New York, 1971.

OLIVIER, EUGÈNE, GEORGES HERMAL AND R. DE ROTON. *Manuel de l'amateur de reliures armoriées françaises*. 29 vols. Paris, 1924-1935.

PRIDEAUX, SARAH T. *Bookbinders and their craft*. New York, 1903.

———. *Modern bookbindings; their design and decoration*. London, 1906.

La reliure originale française; [an exhibition at the] Museum of Contemporary Crafts organized under the patronage of the Société de la Reliure Originale. New York, 1964.

RICCI, SEYMOUR DE. *Census of medieval and Renaissance manuscripts in the United States and Canada, by Seymour de Ricci, with the assistance of W. J. Wilson*. 3 vols. Reprint. New York, 1961.

A rod for the back of the binder; some considerations of bookbinding with reference to the ideals of the Lakeside Press. Chicago, 1929.

ROYLANCE, DALE R. "The Altschul collection: the arts of the French book, 1838-1967." *Yale University Library gazette*, vol. 44, no. 2, October 1969.

SHIPMAN, C. (trans. & rev.) *Researches concerning Jean Grolier, his life and his library. With a partial catalogue of his books by A. J. V. Le Roux de Lincy*. Edited by Baron R. Portalis. New York, 1907.

SMITH, PHILIP. "Designing for bookbinders—part 2." *Designer bookbinders review 10*. Autumn 1977.

———. *The Lord of the rings and other bindings of P. Smith*. London, 1970.

———. *New directions in bookbinding*. London and New York, 1974.

SOMMERLAD, MICHAEL J. *Scottish 'wheel' and 'herring-bone' bindings in The Bodleian Library, an illustrated handlist*. Oxford, 1967.

STONEHOUSE, JOHN H. *The story of the great Omar bound by Francis Longinus Sangorski and its romantic loss*. London, 1933.

Thomas W. Patterson, bookbinder; [an exhibition held at] the Hunt Institute for Botanical Documentation. Pittsburgh, 1972.

THOMPSON, ELBERT A. AND LAWRENCE S. THOMPSON. *Fine binding in America; the story of The Club Bindery*. Urbana, Ill., 1956.

THOMPSON, LAWRENCE S. "Fritz Eberhardt, American binder." *American book collector*, vol. 8, no. 10, June 1958.

TITCOMBE, MARIANNE F. *The bookbinding career of Rachel McMasters Miller Hunt*. Pittsburgh, 1974.

Verslag omtrent de Koninklijke Bibliotheek. The Hague, 1970.

(Victoria & Albert Museum.) *Two modern binders: William Matthews & Edgar Mansfield; [an exhibition held at the] . . . in association with Designer Bookbinders*. Introduction by Bernard C. Middleton. London, 1978.

26. *Sangorski and Sutcliffe, ca. 1906-1923*

32. *Henri Creuzevault, 20th century*

36. *Jean Gunner, 1978*

49. *Pierre-Lucien Martin, 1962*

74. *Sangorski and Sutcliffe, 1912*

77. *Philip Smith, 1974-1975*

69

80. *Jean Gunner, 1979*

84. *Paul Bonet, 1964*

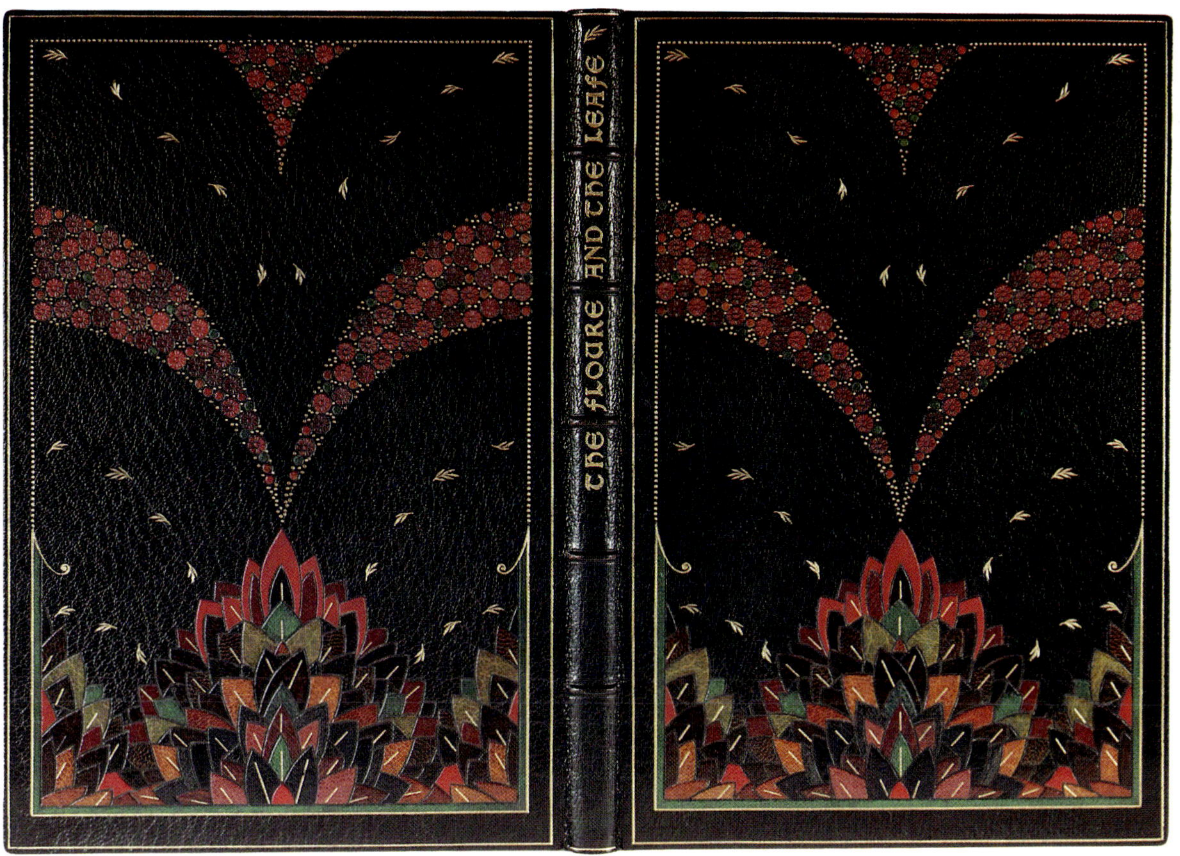

85. *Alfred de Sauty, ca. 1926*

87. *Trevor Jones, 1976*

90. *Edgar Mansfield, 1964*

92. *Roger Powell, 1963*

93. *Sybil Pye, 1939*

94. *Ivor Robinson, 1971–1972*

75

96. *Philip Smith, 1967-1968*

5. *Blind-tooled binding with panel stamp, ca. 1574*

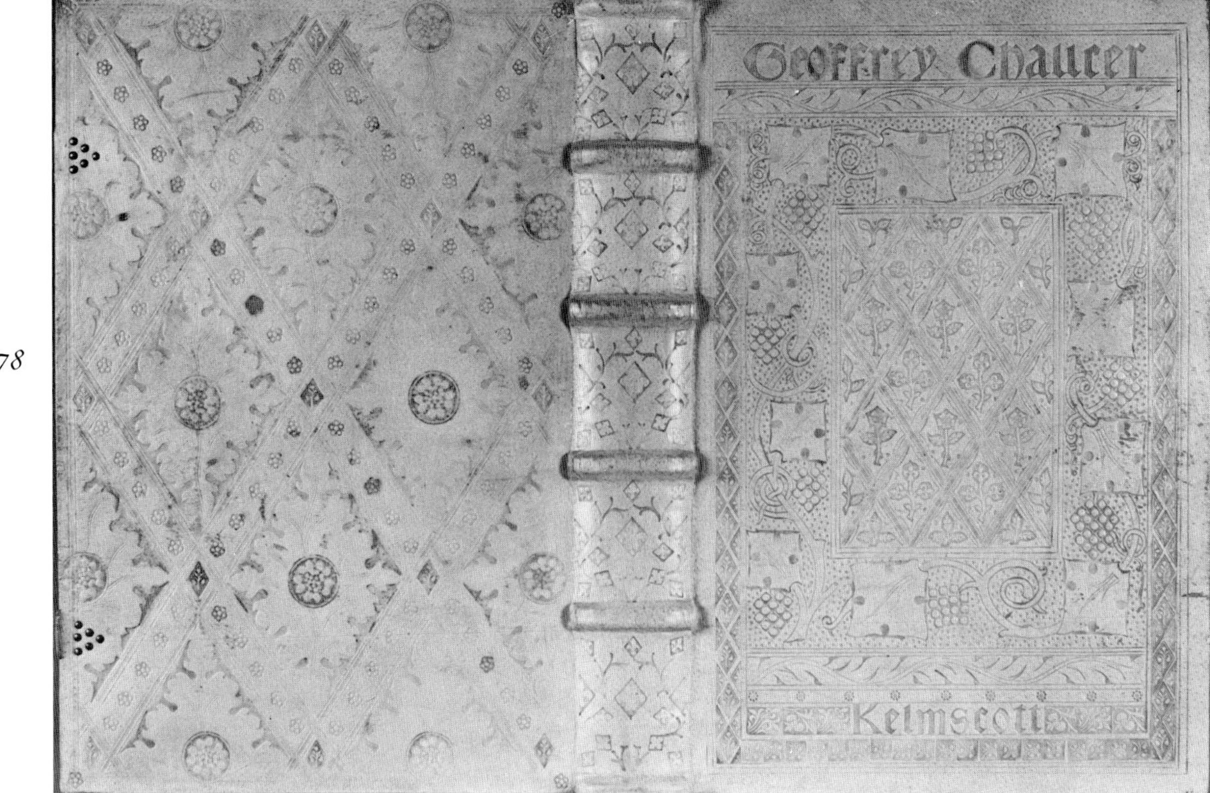

6. *Doves Bindery, 1897*

7. *Blind-tooled quarter pigskin binding, ca. early 20th century*

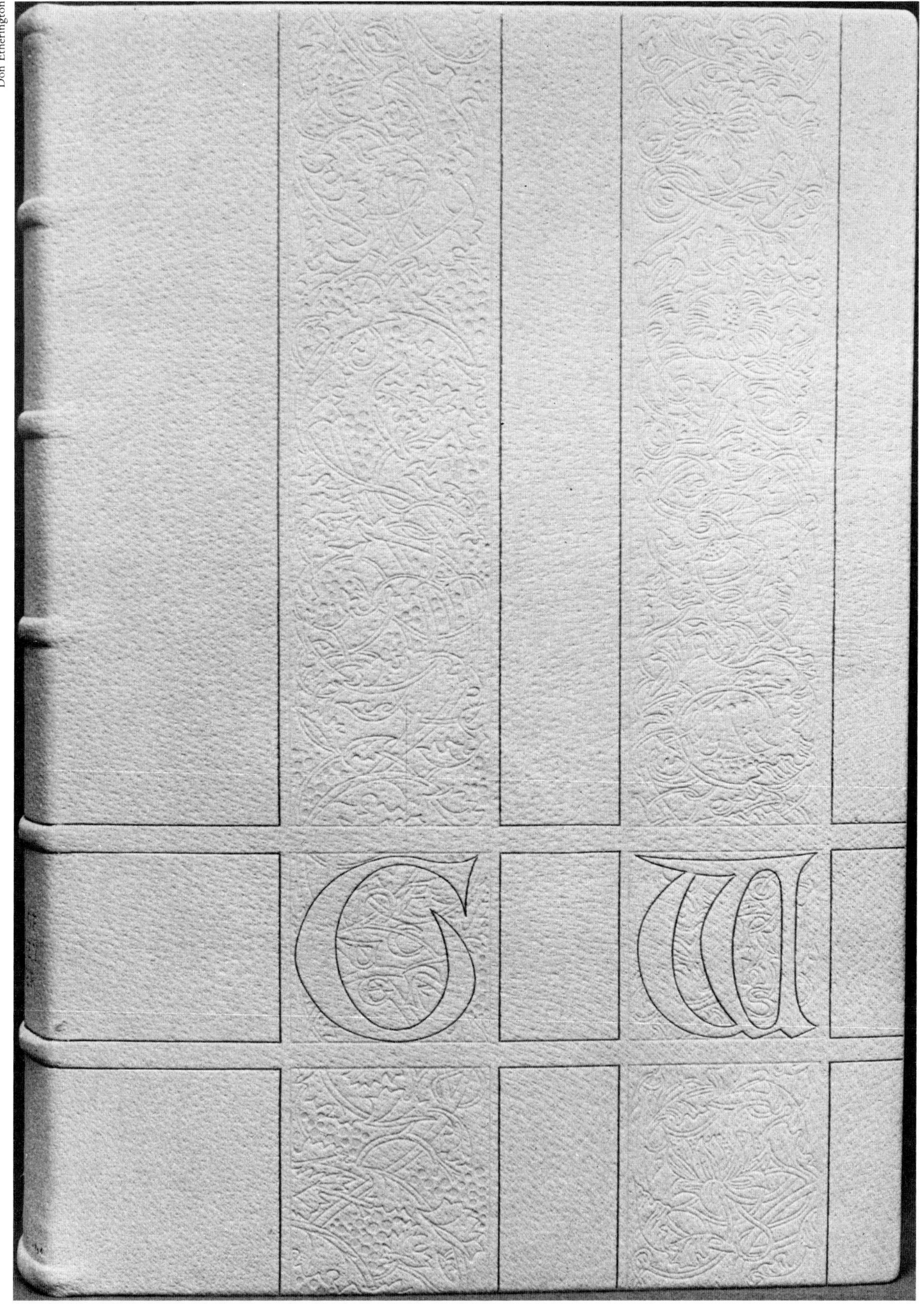

8. *Don Etherington, 1977*

9. *Blind-stamped binding, ca. early 20th century*

10. *Carolyn Horton & Associates, 1977*

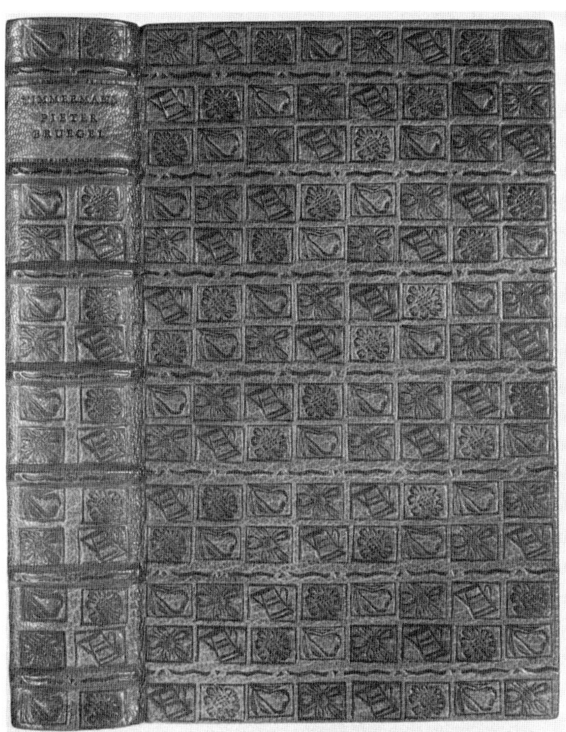

11. *Fritz Eberhardt, 1956*

 82

12. *Gold-stamped vellum binding, ca. 1580*

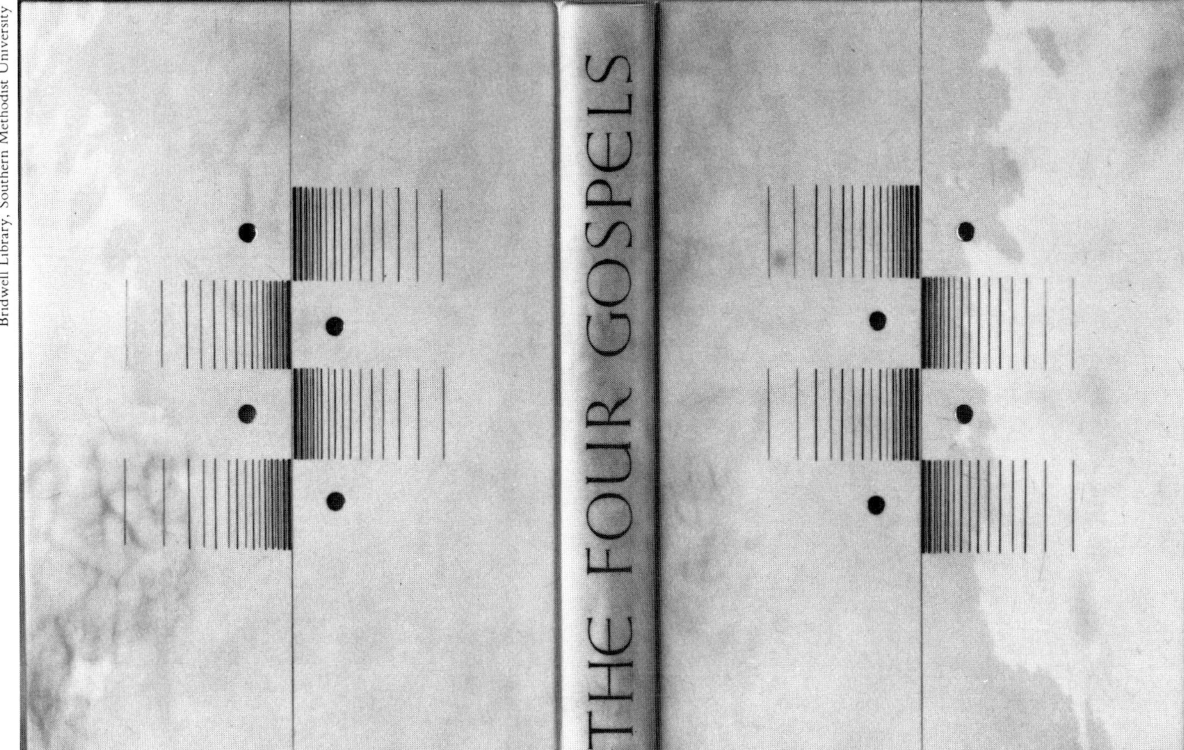

13. *Sydney M. Cockerell and Joan Rix Tebbutt, 1976*

15. *Club Bindery, 1906*

16. *Rachel McMasters Miller Hunt, 1917-1918*

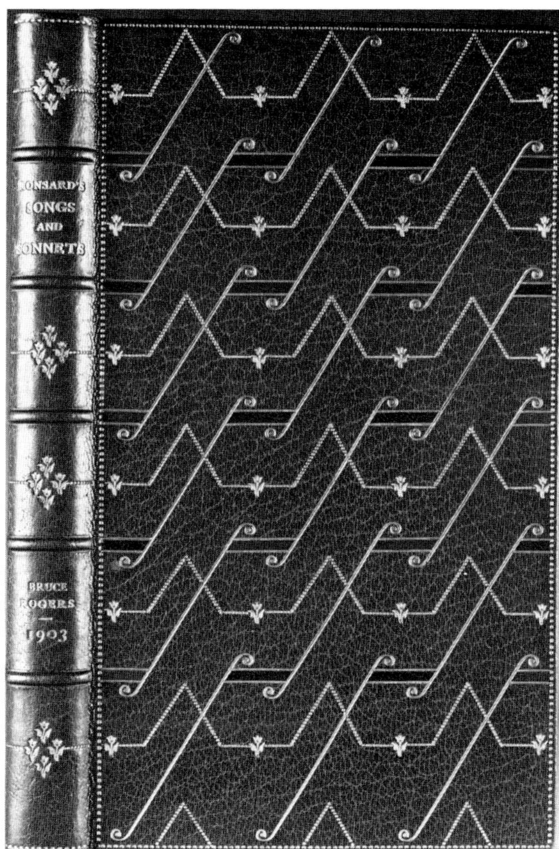

17. *Alfred de Sauty, 1929*

86

18. *Claude de Piques?, ca. 1540*

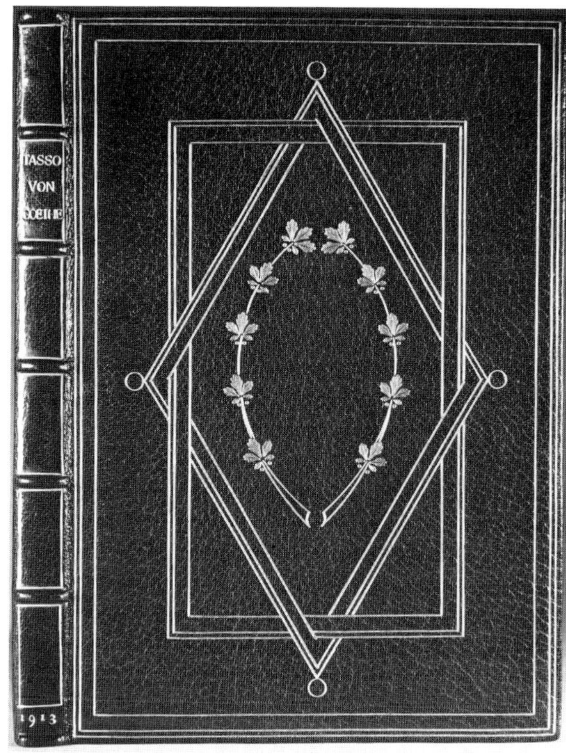

19. *Doves Bindery*, *1919*

20. *Jean Gunner*, *1964*

23. *Rachel McMasters Miller Hunt, 1911*

24. *Clovis Eve?, late 16th to early 17th century*

22. *Charles McLeisch, 1909*

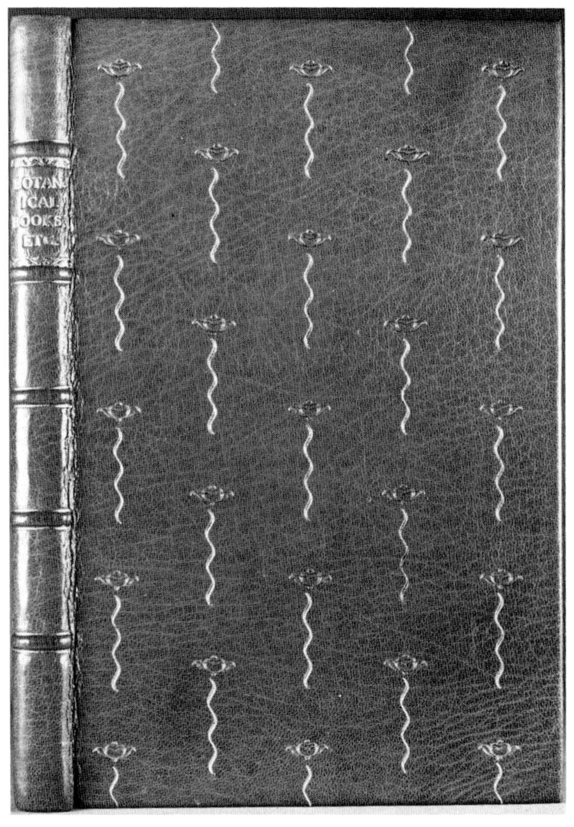

27. *Thomas W. Patterson, 1959*

25. *Thomas J. Cobden-Sanderson, 1885*

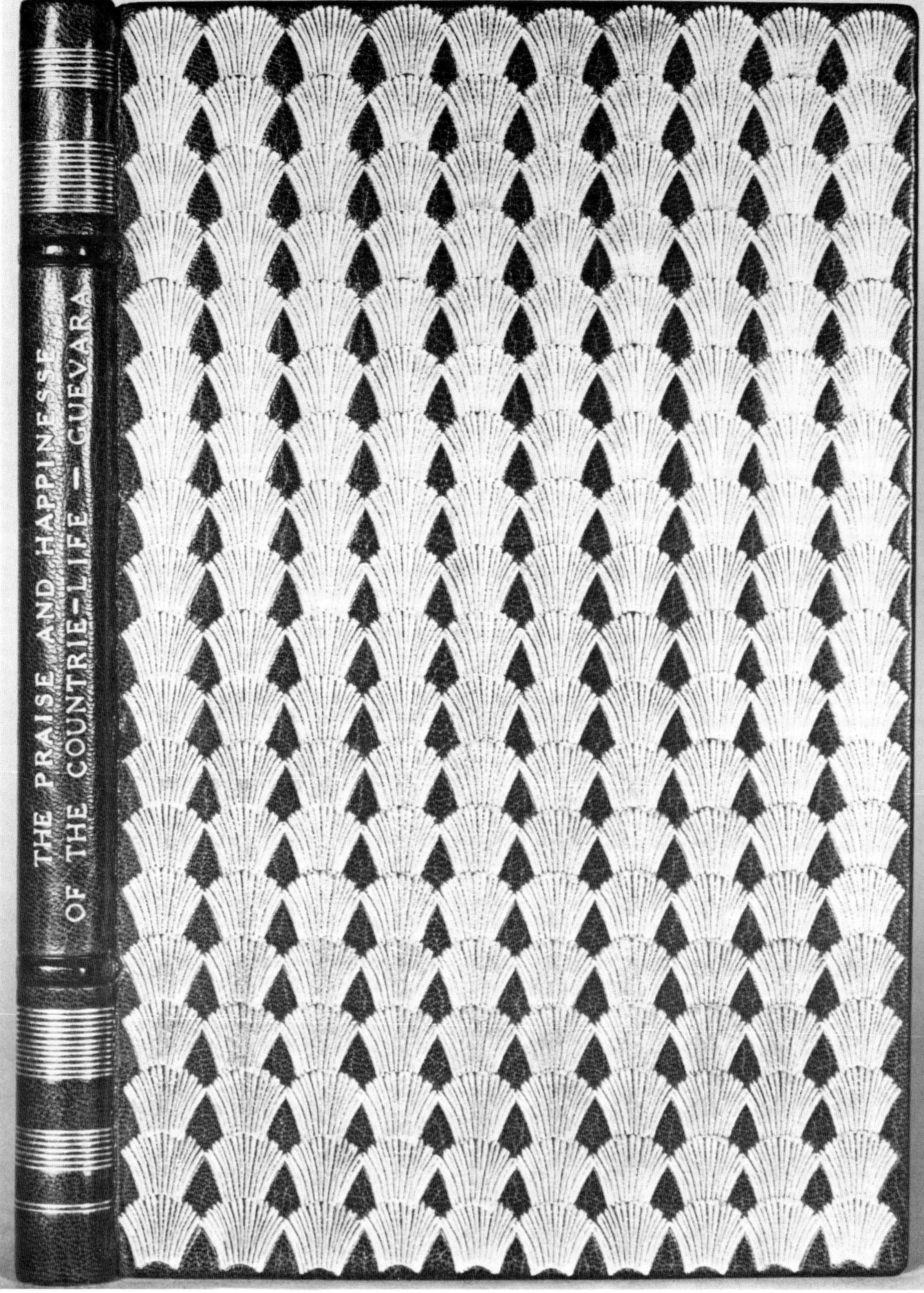

28. *William Matthews, 1970*

29. *Michael Wilcox, 1979*

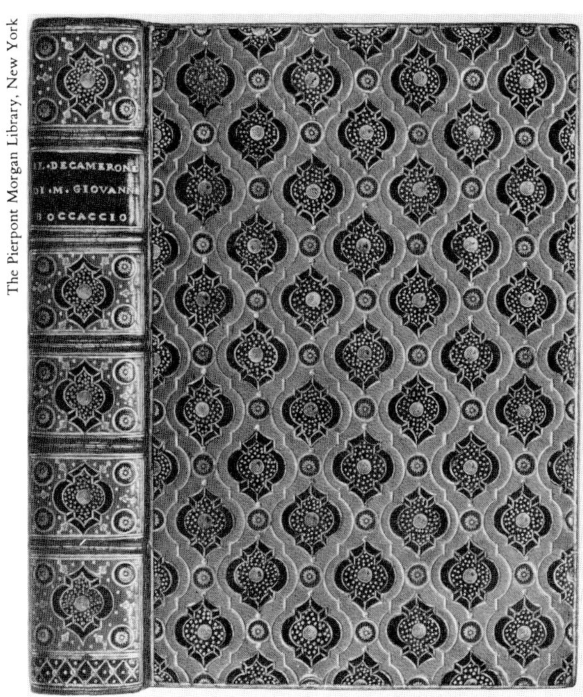

30. *Antoine-Michael Padeloup, ca. 1730-1740*

93

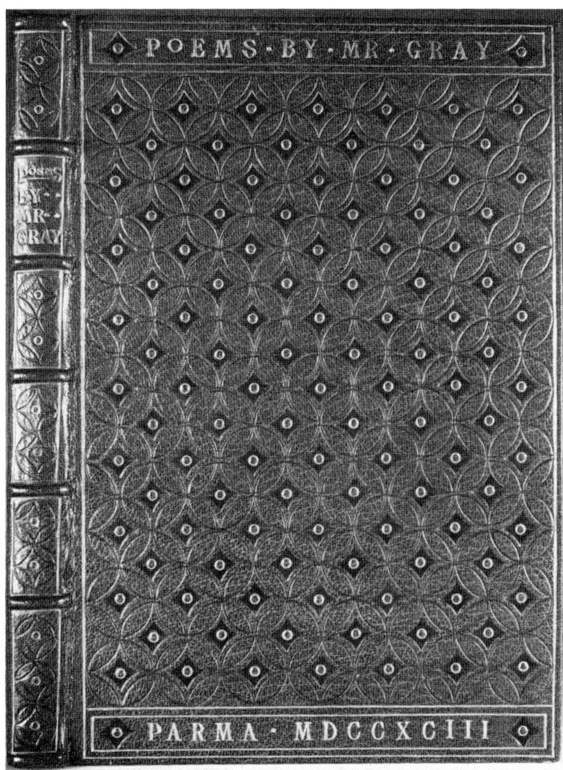

31. *Rachel McMasters Miller Hunt, 1918*

33. *The Queen's Binder, ca. 1673*

34. *Jean Gunner, 1979*

35. *Cottage roof binding, 17th century*

37. *Ivor Robinson, 1976*

38. *Restoration panel binding, ca. 1717*

39. *William Matthews, 1969*

97

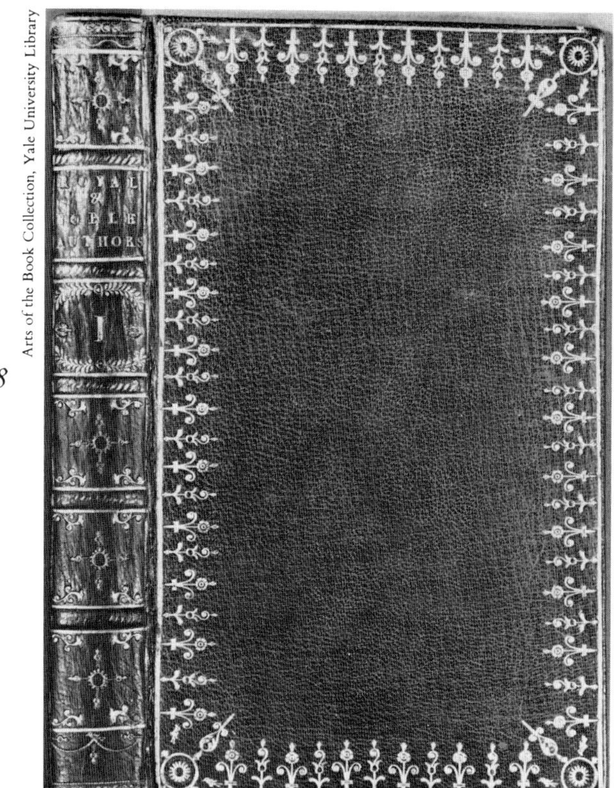

40. *Roger Payne, ca. 1764*

41. *Nicolas Derome, ca. 1760*

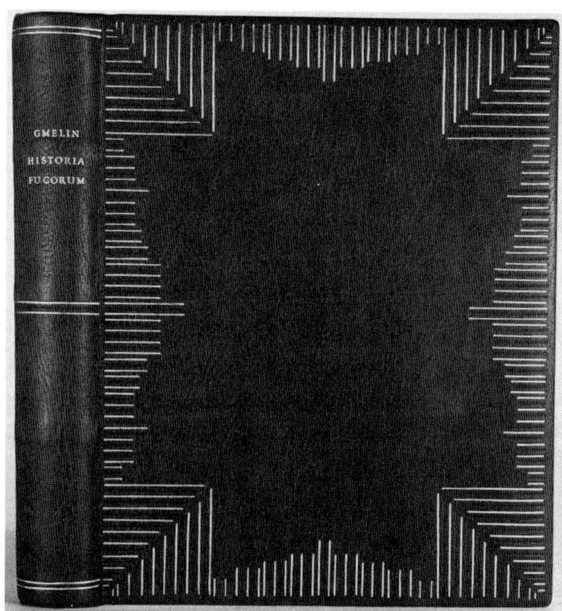

43. *Jean Gunner, 1979*

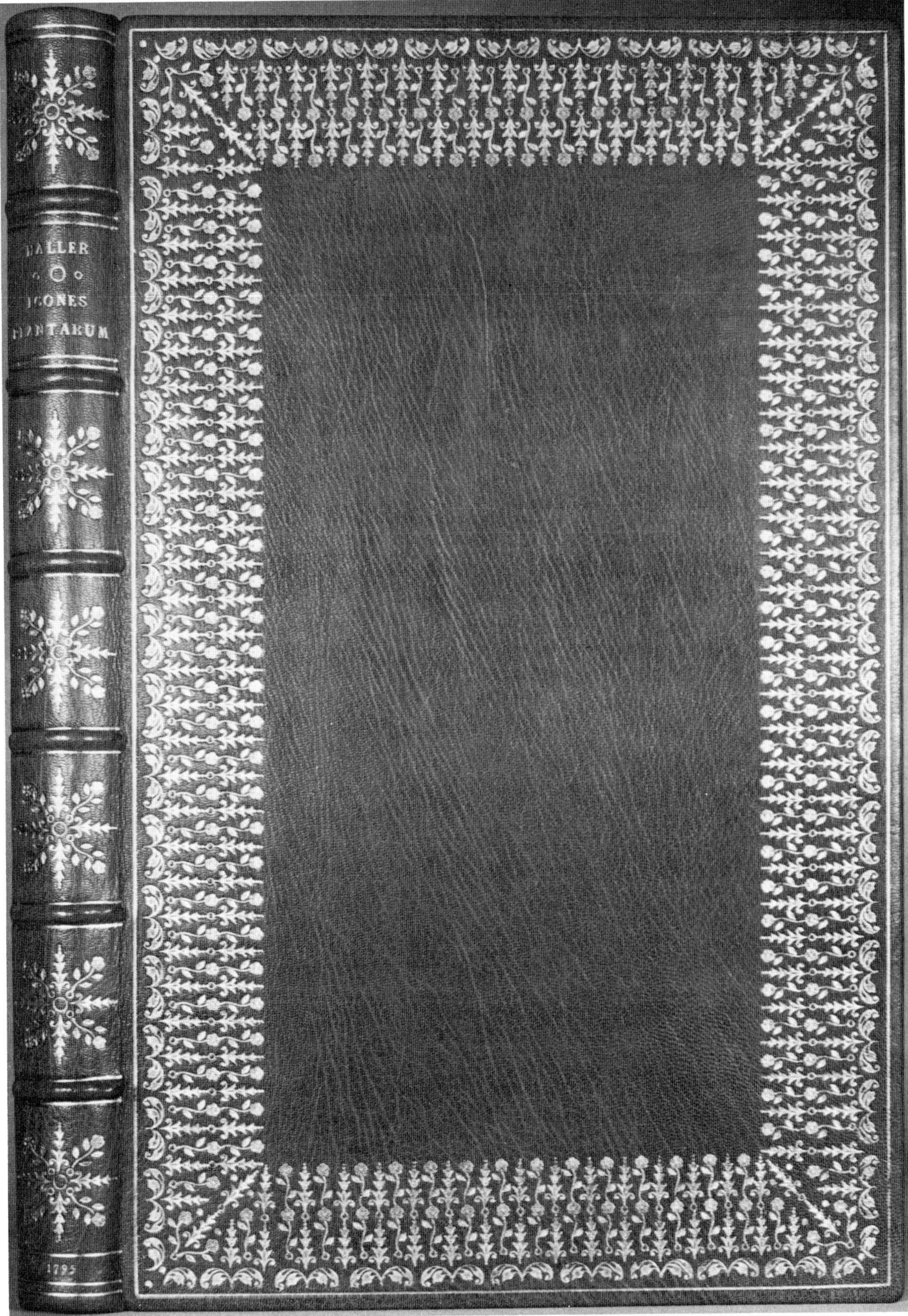

42. *Jean Gunner, 1979*

44. *Doves Bindery, 1908*

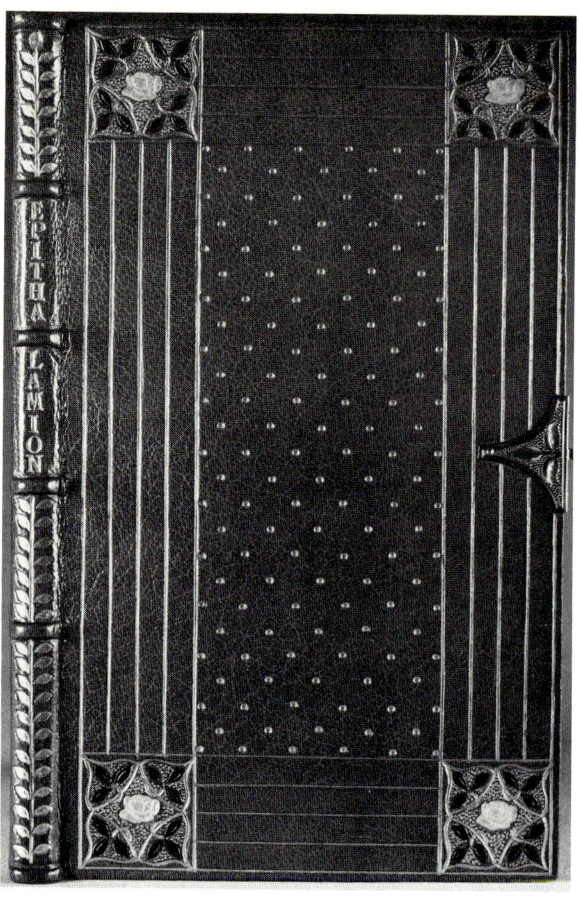

45. *Rachel McMasters Miller Hunt, 1910*

46. *John F. Grabau, 1930*

47. *Bernard C. Middleton, 1978*

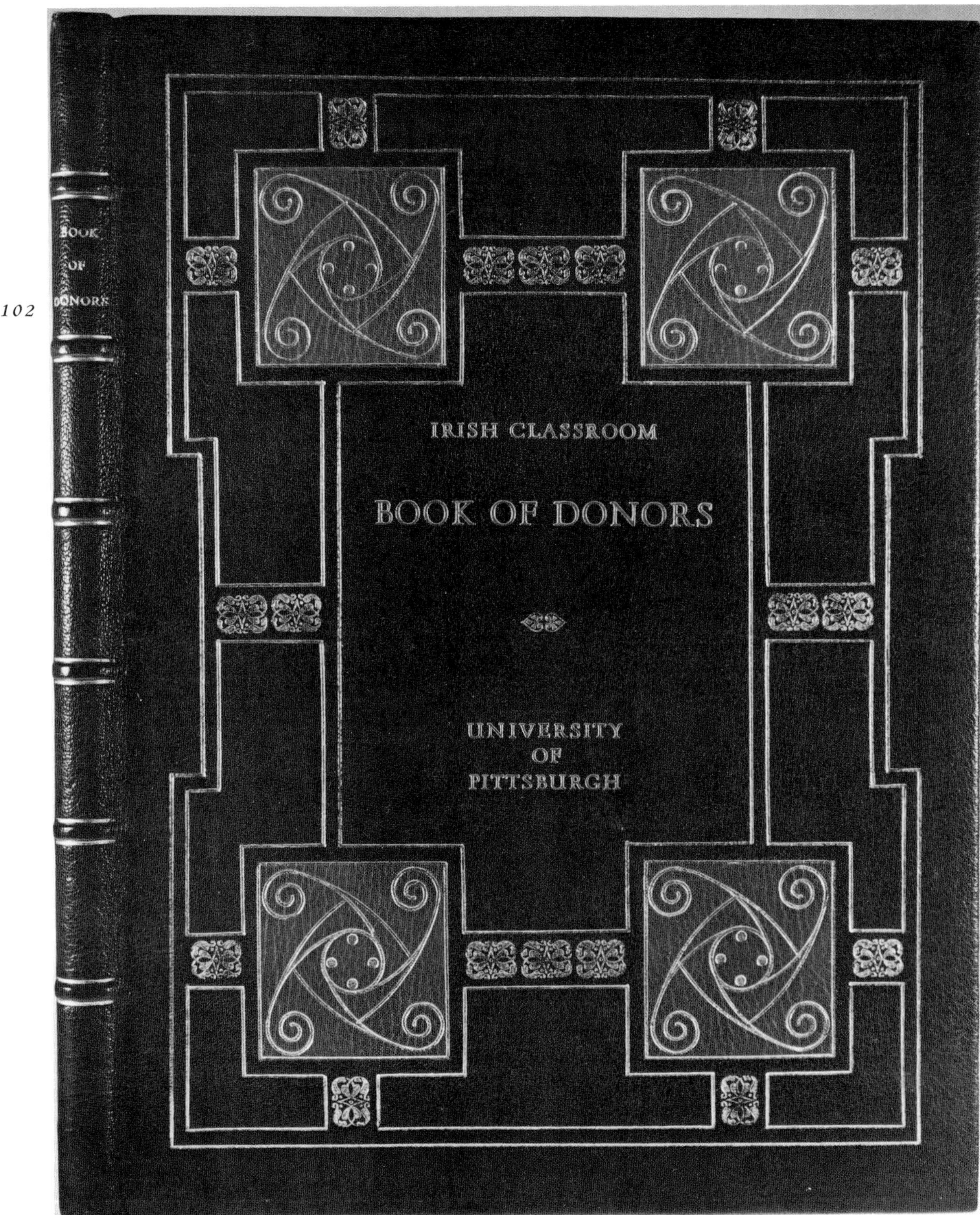

48. *Thomas W. Patterson, 1957–1958*

50. *Sprinkled panel binding, ca. 18th century*

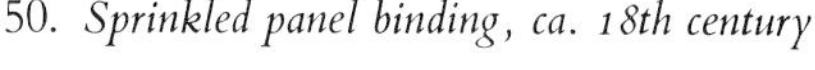

51. *Rivière and Son, 20th century*

52. *Rachel McMasters Miller Hunt, 1909*

53. *Stamped center medallion binding, ca. 1555*

54. *Douglas Cockerell, 1900*

55. *Jean Gunner, 1978*

57. *Ramage, early 20th century*

58. *Jean Gunner, 1978*

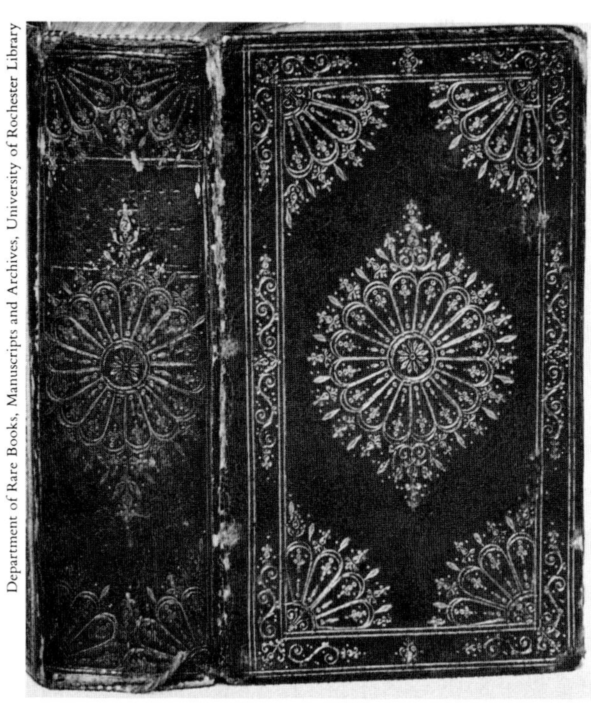

56. *Tooled fan binding, ca. 1600–1650*

59. *Paul Bonet, 1946*

60. *Dandini arms, ca. 1575*

61. *Arms of Jacques Auguste de Thou, 1608–1617*

62. *Eve style, ca. 1665-1715*

63. *Arms of Baron Stuart de Rothesay, 18th century*

64. *Farragher and Linder, ca. 1806-1817*

65. *Thouvenin, ca. 1826-1830*

66. *Armand, ca. 1929*

67. *American Historical Company, 1965*

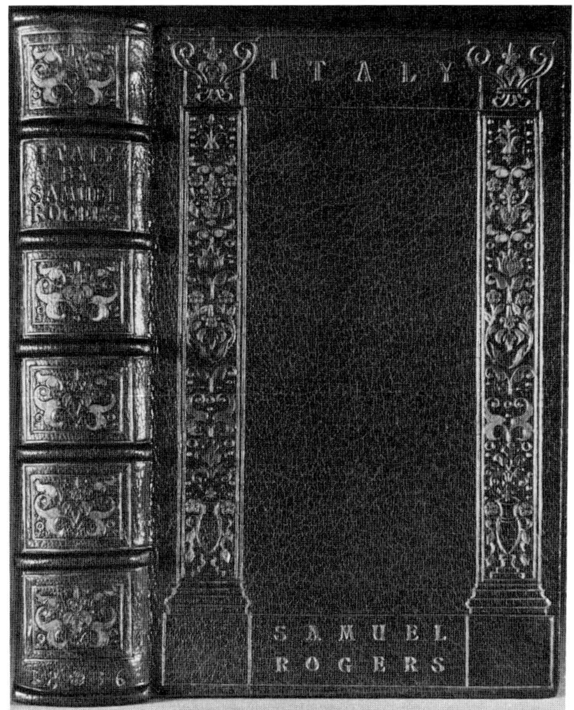

70. *Rachel McMasters Miller Hunt, 1916*

71. *Jean Gunner, 1979*

72. *Edwards of Halifax, ca. 1780*

73. *Kelliegram, 19th century*

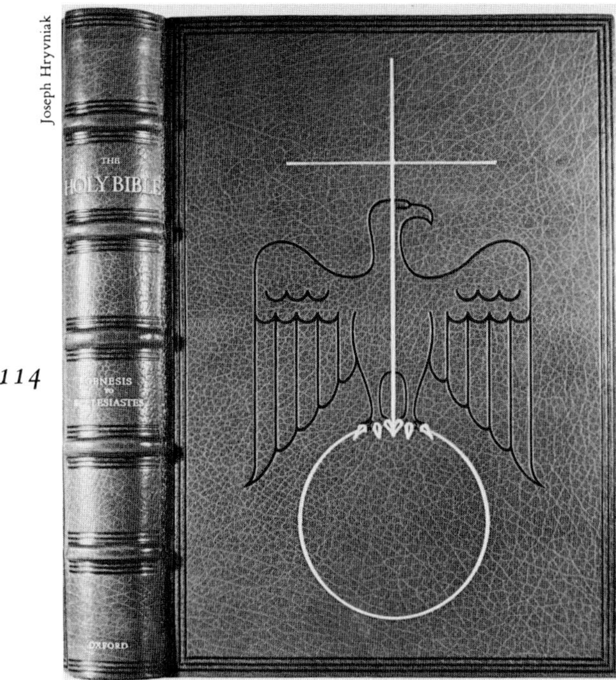

75. *Rivière and Son, 1935*

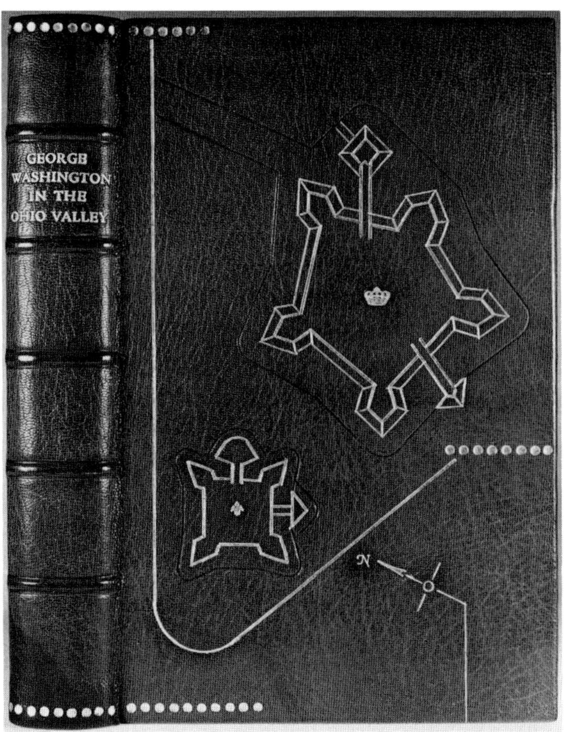

76. *Thomas W. Patterson, 1956*

78. *Gérard Charriere, 1977*

116

79. *Bernard C. Middleton, 1977*

83. *Rose Adler, 1931*

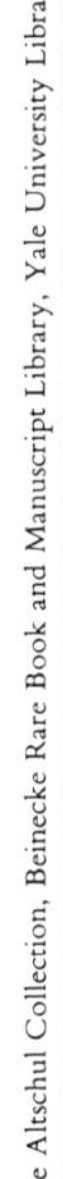

81. *Henri Marius-Michel, ca. 1906–1925*

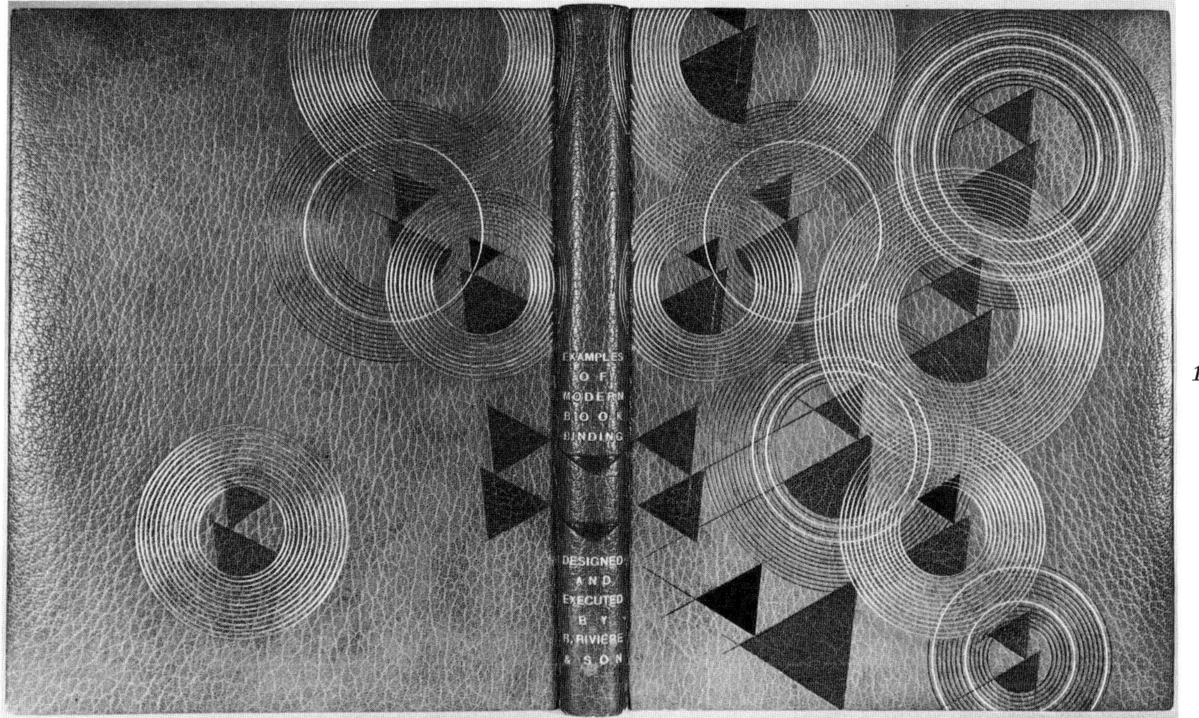

82. *Pierre Legrain, ca. 1919*

86. *Alfred de Sauty, 1930*

120

88. *Georges Leroux, 1964*

122

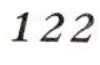

89. *Edgar Mansfield, 1937*

91. *William Matthews, 1975*

124

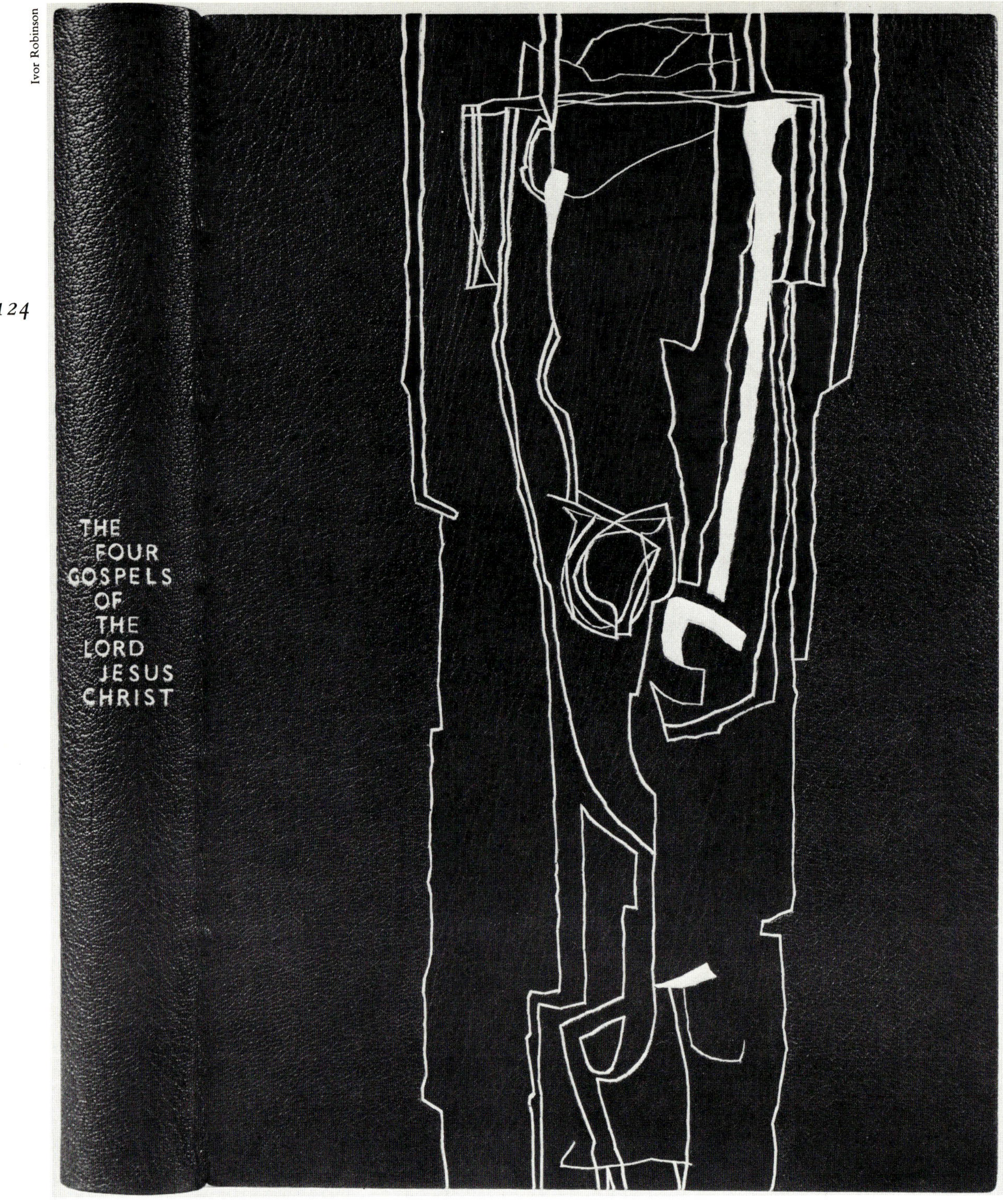

95. *Ivor Robinson, 1975*

INDEX OF AUTHORS, ANONYMOUS TITLES,
BINDERS AND PREVIOUS OWNERS MENTIONED
IN CATALOGUE ENTRIES

Numbers in italics indicate entries for bindings executed by the parties referenced.

129